THE TAXATION OF CORPORATIONS

IN

MASSACHUSETTS

BY

HARRY G. FRIEDMAN

AMS PRESS
NEW YORK

COLUMBIA UNIVERSITY
STUDIES IN THE
SOCIAL SCIENCES

74

The Series was formerly known as
Studies in History, Economics and Public Law.

Reprinted with the permission of Columbia University Press
From the edition of 1907, New York
First AMS EDITION published 1968
Manufactured in the United States of America

Library of Congress Catalogue Card Number: 76-76678

AMS PRESS, INC.
NEW YORK, N. Y. 10003

PREFACE

THE desirability of presenting in concrete form the significance of the taxation of corporations is, in the author's opinion, justification for devoting this monograph to the taxation of corporations in a single state. The industrial character of Massachusetts, together with its extended history in the taxation of corporations, gives peculiar fitness to the state here chosen. The writer has sought to trace the historical development of the corporation taxes and to indicate their fiscal importance. He has, however, aimed to emphasize the present situation, and to present the significance of taxation in general for corporate activity. The reader whose interest is primarily in the present development is referred to the part of this work beginning with chapter four and the concluding sections of chapters two and three.

The author was not aware that Professor Bullock contemplated the study of the general subject of corporation taxes in Massachusetts, and this monograph was virtually completed when Professor Bullock's article appeared in the *Quarterly Journal of Economics* for February. Obligation is acknowledged at the proper places in the notes. The writer, in submitting this work, trusts that there is still room for this more extended study.

The writer is glad to avail himself of this opportunity to express his gratitude to those who have helped him in his work. He is under great obligation to Mr. C. B.

Tillinghast, librarian of the Massachusetts State Library, for furnishing him with documents that have facilitated his study. For similar kindness he is indebted to Mr. L. A. Phillips. To Professor H. B. Gardner he is under obligation for bibliographical assistance. The author's thanks are due to Professor H. R. Seager, at whose suggestion and encouragement the study of taxation in Massachusetts was undertaken. To Professor H. L. Moore, who has had the trying task of reading this monograph in proof, the author feels deep gratitude. Above all he is under obligation to Professor E. R. A. Seligman.

H. G. F.

COLUMBIA UNIVERSITY, 1907.

CONTENTS

CHAPTER I

TAXATION OF CORPORATIONS BEFORE THE CIVIL WAR

PAGE

I. Growth of corporate activity 11
II. Taxation of corporate shares under the general corporation tax. 13
III. Tax on banks 19
IV. Taxation of insurance companies 21
V. Taxation of deposits in savings banks 22

CHAPTER II

TAXATION OF CORPORATIONS FROM THE CIVIL WAR TO THE PRESENT TIME

I. Growth of expenditures as a result of the war 24
II. Consequent development of the corporation taxes 25
III. Legal basis of the corporation taxes 27
IV. Administration of the corporation taxes 32
V. Fiscal importance of the corporation taxes 34
    1. For state revenue 35
    2. For municipal revenue 37
    3. As compared with property and other taxes 39
VI. Economic importance of corporation taxes 42

CHAPTER III

THE GENERAL CORPORATION TAX

I. The general corporation tax and the earlier tax on corporate shares 45
II. Features of the general corporation tax 46
    1. Corporations to which the tax is applicable 46
    2. Basis of the tax 47
    3. Rate of the tax 49
    4. Distribution of the proceeds 50

PAGE

III. The general property tax and its relation to the taxation of
    corporations 52
  1. Real estate 52
  2. Personal estate 52
  3. Assessment of personal estate to individuals and to cor-
    porations 54
  4. Method of assessment and results 55
IV. Working of the general corporation tax 56
  1. Results 56
  2. Views of tax commissions 58
  3. Recent dissatisfaction with the tax in connection with :
      (1) Public service corporations 59
      (2) Business corporations 60
V. Importance of the general corporation tax for various groups
    of corporations 61
VI. Criticism of the general corporation tax 62
  1. The basis of the tax 62
      (1) Taxation of capital stock alone 63
      (2) Other criticisms 64
  2. Results 65
  3. Distribution of the proceeds 68
      (1) As between state and municipalities 68
      (2) As between municipalities 68
      (3) Results 69
      (4) Basis for reform 73

CHAPTER IV

TAXATION OF BUSINESS CORPORATIONS

I. Theory of the general corporation tax 77
II. Taxation of business corporations under the general corpora-
    tion tax 78
  1. Relative advantages for taxation of individuals, domestic
    corporations and foreign corporations 79
  2. Growth of foreign corporations 80
  3. Situation in 1901 81
  4. Changes in the tax law and their purpose 83
III. Taxation under the Business Corporation Law of 1903 85
  1. Provisions of the law 85
      (1) Significance 87
      (2) Effect 88
  2. Criticism 92

PAGE

(1) From the point of view of the taxation of :
    (a) Property 92
    (b) Income 93
(2) Other criticisms 94
IV. Taxation of corporations to engage in business outside of the
state 95
V. Taxations of foreign corporations 98
VI. Incorporation fees 100

CHAPTER V

TAXATION OF PUBLIC-SERVICE CORPORATIONS

I. Various policies adopted by the state in taxing public-service
   corporations 102
II. General corporation tax and public-service corporations . . 105
  1. Criticism 105
  2. Reform 106
III. Fiscal importance of the corporation tax on public-service
   corporations 108
IV. Taxation of street railways 111
  1. Historical :
    (1) Growth of street railways 111
    (2) Criticisms of the general corporation tax 112
    (3) Changes in the law :
      (a) The distribution of the tax 113
      (b) Special franchise tax 114
  2. Present situation :
    (1) Summary of the law 115
    (2) Corporation tax and local taxes 117
    (3) Inadequacy of the present basis of taxation . . . 117
    (4) Inequality of present method of taxation 118
    (5) Relation of taxes to earnings 119
    (6) Summary 121
V. Taxation of railroads 122
  1. Corporation tax and local taxes 122
  2. Inadequacy of the present basis of the tax 123
  3. Results of the taxation of railroads in Massachusetts as
    compared with taxation in other states 127
  4. Taxation of other transportation agencies 128
VI. Taxation of gas companies.
  1. Corporation tax and local taxes 130
  2. Relation of taxes to earnings 130

PAGE

VII. Taxation of electric light companies 131
    1. Corporation tax and local taxes 131
    2. Relation of taxes to earnings 132
VIII. Taxation of telegraph and telephone companies 132
IX. Taxation of other public-service corporations 135

CHAPTER VI

TAXATION OF FINANCIAL CORPORATIONS

I. Policies of the state in taxing of financial corporations . . 136
II. Taxation of trust companies 137
    1. On capital stock 138
    2. On deposits and on property held in trust 139
III. Taxation of banks 141
    1. Development of present method 142
    2. Present method and its operation 144
    3. Relation of taxes to earnings 147
    4. Significance of the tax on trust companies and banks . 148
IV. Taxation of saving banks 149
    1. Historical 149
    2. Present significance 152
V. Taxation of fire and marine insurance companies 155
    1. Massachusetts stock companies 156
    2. Massachusetts mutual companies 157
    3. Foreign companies 158
VI. Taxation of life insurance companies 160

CHAPTER VII

SUMMARY AND CONCLUSION

I. Historical development of the corporation taxes 163
II. Influences in the development 168
III. Present significance 170
IV. Criticism 173
V. Relation of the government to corporations, and its signifi-
    cance for the taxation of corporations 176
APPENDIX—Street Railway Taxes 178

CHAPTER I

THE TAXATION OF CORPORATIONS IN MASSACHUSETTS BEFORE THE CIVIL WAR

CORPORATE activity in industry begins in Massachusetts immediately after the close of the Revolutionary War. The first important corporation was the Massachusetts Bank, organized in 1784.[1] Before the completion of the century, corporations had been chartered not only for public service enterprises, like the building of canals, bridges, aqueducts and turnpikes, and financial undertakings in banking and insurance, but also for carrying on manufacturing. In the course of the first quarter of the nineteenth century corporate activity in manufactures, particularly in the textile industry, grew rapidly. In 1816 the first savings bank was chartered. To the first quarter of the century belongs also the first gas light company. In 1830 the first railroad was chartered, and in 1853 the first street railway. Corporate activity had become sufficiently general by the middle of the century to cause the enactment, in 1851, of the first general corporation law.[2]

[1] The Proprietors of Boston Pier or the Long Wharf had been incorporated in 1772. Cf. A. M. Davis, "Corporations in the Days of the Colony," *Publications of the Colonial Society of Massachusetts*, vol. i, pp. 212, 213; S. E. Baldwin, "American Business Corporations before 1789," *Annual Report of the American Historical Association*, 1902, vol. i, pp. 257, 267.

[2] Cf. James R. Carret, "Taxation of Franchises in Massachusetts," *Municipal Affairs*, iv, pp. 506–7; *Sixteenth Annual Report of the Massachusetts Bureau of Statistics of Labor*, pp. 173, 175; *Report of the Committee on Corporation Laws*, 1903, pp. 16, 17.

In the early sixties corporations had become so important as to create dissatisfaction with the inadequacy of the general property tax for reaching their property. The companies then assessed for taxation had a capital as follows:

	Banks.	Insurance Companies.	Industrial Corporations.	Railroads.
1860....	$64,995,000	$7,381,600	$58,888,430	$50,108,300
1861....	66,395,000	7,446,777	62,406,380	

In addition, savings banks held deposits amounting to $43,972,537 in 1860, and $45,016,470 in 1861.[1] Even as assessed by the inefficient methods then in use corporate property formed a large percentage of the total amount of property taxed. According to the assessors' returns there were taxed, in addition to the real estate and machinery of corporations, the following amounts:[2]

	Bank Shares.	Shares in Insurance Companies.	Shares in Industrial Corporations.	Railroad Shares.	Savings Bank Deposits.
1860....	$38,374,649	$7,654,148	$10,571,378	$12,581,689	$8,847,588
1861....	36,093,801	6,963,840	8,210,934	19,339,459	9,655,796

The total valuation for the state in 1861 was $861,547,-000; the valuation of personal estate alone $309,397,000. In this total for personal estate were included the value of shares in excess of the value of the real estate and machinery of corporations, amounting in 1861 to $70,-600,000, and savings bank deposits amounting to $9,655,-000, together $80,263,000. This sum constituted little

[1] *Abstracts of the Returns of Assessors relating to the Assessment of Taxes on the Shares of Corporations and Deposits in Savings Institutions*, for 1860 and 1861. Boston, 1861 and 1862, pp. 261 and 305 respectively.

[2] *Ibid.*

less than ten per cent of the entire valuation of property, and more than twenty-five per cent of all personal property assessed in the state.

I. *The Taxation of Corporate Shares under the General Property Tax.*—The present system of taxing corporations had a twofold origin, the general property tax and a special business tax imposed on banks. It is the purpose of the succeeding pages first to trace the steps in the development of the taxation of corporate property under the general property tax, before the Civil War, and then to discuss briefly the bank tax, and the other special corporation taxes of this period.

In the act prescribing the returns of the assessors for the state valuation in 1792, we find the first mention of corporate stock, the attention of the assessors being called to stock in banks.[1] In 1801 " bank shares or property held in any incorporate bridges or turnpike roads" are included in the list of taxables,[2] and in 1805 " shares in any other incorporated company possessing taxable property" are added.[3] The tax act of 1822 provides for the taxation of " all bank and insurance stock and shares or property in any incorporated company possessing taxable property, according to the value thereof."[4] The Revised Statutes, the first general code adopted in 1835, included corporate shares under personal estate, and speaks specifically of " stocks in turnpikes, bridges, and all moneyed corporations."[5] The valuation act of 1840 makes special mention of railroad shares.[6] The provision of the Revised Statutes was repeated in the General

---

[1] 1792, c. 17; see also 1793, c. 9A.

[2] 1800, c. 77, § 2.   [3] 1804, c. 144, § 12.

[4] 1821, c. 107.   [5] *Revised Statutes*, c. 7, § 4.

[6] 1840, c. 78, § 1.

Statutes (1859).[1]   The growth of corporate property was thus reflected in the tax laws.

It seems that at the outset the practice was to tax corporations for all their property and also to tax shareholders again for the value of their shares.   In 1813 the question of the proper manner of taxing corporations was brought before the Supreme Judicial Court, and it was decided that corporations could be taxed only for real estate, and not for their personal property.[2]   "The tax is always supposed to be assessed upon persons, for and according to the value of the estate, real and personal, owned or possessed by them respectively," was the view of the court, and corporations were not persons for taxation.   For real estate an exception was to be made, because real estate was included in the state valuation of the city or town.   The doctrine was thus established that corporations are not to be taxed for their personalty unless the property is made specifically taxable to the corporation.[3]

Double taxation was, however, only partially obviated by this decision, as there was no provision for deducting the value of the real estate from the value of the shares in taxing the stockholders.   In the assessment law of 1832 a method was devised by which the double taxation of the property of manufacturing corporations was avoided. Machinery and real estate were taxed to the corporation, and at the same time the assessors were required, in taxing the shareholders, to deduct from the value of their shares a corresponding proportion of the value of the

[1] *General Statutes*, c. 11, § 4; see particularly 184 Mass. 460.

[2] Salem Iron Factory *vs.* Danvers, 10 Mass. 514; *cf.* also 17 Mass. 461.

[3] This doctrine is often repeated in court decisions.   See in particular 104 Mass. 587–588, and 184 Mass. 460.

real estate and machinery of the corporation.[1] With little more than a change to centralized administration, the law as established in 1832 became the general corporation tax law of 1864 and 1865.

Corporations other than manufacturing companies, the court held, were not liable to taxation for personal property. These were chiefly banks and insurance companies having a capital stock. For their personalty they could be reached only through the tax on their shares. They were, of course, taxed on their real estate, but no provision seems to have been made for deducting the real estate from the shares. As such corporations, however, held little real estate, the burden of double taxation could not have been very heavy. Mutual corporations, having no shares, such as savings banks and insurance companies, were exempt entirely on their personal estate.[2]

In the taxation of public-service corporations the notable feature is the exemption from taxation not only of their personal estate but in a great measure of their real estate. This was the practice for canals, bridges, turnpikes, highways and their incidents, and for railroads.[3] The exemption was not based on statute but on inference from the right of eminent domain conferred on this class of corporations. Their works were regarded as "public easements," and as such exempt, like public buildings. Railroads, the court held in 1842, were not taxable for a strip of land five rods in width, located for the road, nor for any buildings or structures erected thereon, "reasonably incident to the support of the railroad or to its proper or convenient use for the carriage

[1] 1832, c. 158, § 2. *R. S.*, c. 7, § 10.
[2] 4 Met. 181; 9 Met. 199; 7 Cush. 601.
[3] 4 Met., 564.

of passengers and the transportation of commodities."
"Engine and car houses, depots for the accommodation
of passengers and warehouses," etc., for freight, were
included in the property exempted.   Land and buildings
outside of the five-rod limit were declared, with some
minor exceptions, liable to taxation.[1]   The shares of
these corporations were, however, taxable to the shareholders.   The exemption of real estate from taxation
seems originally to have had for its object the encouragement of a class of enterprises of general benefit to the
public.

The difficulty involved in the mode of taxation out-
lined above was obviously administrative, the difficulty
of reaching effectively intangible property in the hands
of many owners.   This task was the harder, as in the
course of time sworn returns of personal property fell
more and more into disuse.   Hence, beginning with
1843,[2] the Legislature passed a number of acts seeking
to make the law more effective, culminating in the provision contained in the General Statutes, which required
all corporations to report to the assessors of towns and
cities the names and residences of their shareholders,
the number of shares belonging to them, the par and
market value of the shares, the whole amount of capital
stock, and the assessed value of their real estate and
machinery.   Severe penalties were imposed on shareholders who fraudulently transferred their shares in order
to evade taxation, or who failed to give proper information with regard to their residences.[3]

Massachusetts had in 1841 three hundred and five
towns and three cities, and by 1861 the number had

[1] 4 Met. 564; 8 Cush. 237.   [2] 1843, c. 98.
[3] *G. S.*, 68, § 20.

naturally increased. It could not well be expected that the shares should be uniformly valued by the assessors in the different towns, and as a consequence there ensued inequality as between shareholders in the same companies. With ample opportunities for evasion and with no provision for taxing the shares of non-residents, it was impossible to tax all the shares. The outcome may be seen in the returns of the local assessors to the secretary of state for 1860 and 1861. Shares in the same corporation were assessed at different amounts in the different towns, too high in some, too low in others. In some places no deduction was made for property taxed to the corporations. And such inequalities were common.[1]

Various attempts were made to secure fuller and more uniform taxation, especially as taxes increased with the war. Provision was made for correspondence among assessors and more detailed returns from corporations, culminating in the requirement in 1864[2] that corporations transmit to the assessors of each city and town full lists of their shareholders with the amount, the par and market value of their stock, and other necessary information. In 1863 the attempt was made to reach the shares of non-residents by a tax of one-fifteenth of the dividends payable to them. This law, however, was declared unconstitutional.[3] As evidence of the extent of

---

[1] Shares of the Boston and Sandwich Glass Company were assessed at $14.60 in West Roxbury, and $83.00 in Lynn; of the Washington Mills at $11.00 in Boston and $74.00 in Somerville; of the Amesbury Manufacturing Company at from $471.67 to $97.00. Twenty-nine shares of the Lawrence Manufacturing Company were assessed in Medford at $23,200. The same amount of stock was assessed in Milton at $1450. *Abstracts of the Returns of the Assessors, etc.*, 1861, p. 5 *et passim.*

[2] 1864, c. 201.   [3] 1863, c. 236; 11 Allen 268.

evasion, a legislative committee reports that the returns for 1863 showed that in some large corporations not less than one-half of the capital stock was held by non-residents and by parties whose residence was not recorded on the books of the corporation, and that in nearly all corporations a much larger proportion of the capital stock escaped taxation than could reasonably be supposed to belong to persons not residing in the Commonwealth.[1]

The market valuation of shares as the basis for taxation, the deduction of locally taxed real estate and personal property, returns by corporations to the assessors, the essential features of the taxation of corporations having a capital stock divided into shares, are features which reappear in the general corporation tax law of 1864 and 1865, and for the most part are still the characteristics of the Massachusetts system of taxing corporations. The decentralized administration, and the collection of the tax from the shareholder, with the consequent complete escape of non-residents, and the frequent evasion of payment by resident shareholders,—these were the chief faults of the system. To the remedy of these defects the legislation that followed was directed.

For the taxation of foreign corporations, except insurance companies, no special provision was made. Their stock in trade and stock employed in manufacturing were declared taxable in the place where they carried on their business,[2] and this is still law at present. Shares in foreign corporations held by residents in Massachusetts were of course taxable, Massachusetts taxing her citizens for all personal property owned by them outside

---

[1] 1864, *House Documents*, no. 389.
[2] 13 Gray 488. This case was decided in 1859.

of the state.[1]   In a decision in 1866 the court held that
the deduction to be allowed in the assessment of shares
for real estate and machinery did not apply to shares of
foreign corporations.   The practice in Boston, however,
had been to make this deduction from 1832 to 1864.[2]   In
the case of domestic corporations there were some means
of discovering from their returns the owners of the
shares; in the case of foreign corporations, the assessors
had nothing to guide them, except the returns of the tax
payers, and these fell more and more into disuse.

No special provision was made for the taxation of
bonds.   The evasion of the tax on foreign shares and on
bonds we may presume to have been far greater than on
the shares of domestic corporations.   In the taxation of
foreign corporations other than insurance companies, no
change was made until 1903, when there was imposed a
slight excise tax.

II. *The Bank Tax.*—The method of taxing corporation shares described above was merely the application of
the principles of the general property tax to property in
corporations.   There had, however, developed in Massachusetts before the war one important corporation tax
which was a special business tax,—the tax on banks.
This tax was levied on the banks directly, and was independent of and in addition to the tax on shares assessed
to the stockholders under the general property tax.

The bank tax was imposed in 1812.[3]   It levied semi-
annually one-half of one per cent on the amount of capital
actually paid in by the stockholders.   This tax was upheld as an excise on the "commodity" or privilege of
banking, in a decision which afterwards formed the legal

---

[1] 16 Pick. 572.   [2] 12 Allen 316.
[3] 1812, c. 32; 1828, c. 96, § 21; *G. S.*, c. 57, § 89.

basis of the entire structure of corporation taxes.[1]   The
bank tax was evidently regarded as a payment to the
state for the right to circulate bank notes.[2]   Accordingly,
proposals were made to change the basis of the tax from
capital to circulation.   As the issue of bank notes proved
more profitable to country banks than to their city rivals,
the complaint was that the tax resulted in inequality of
burden.   Moreover, it was urged on the one hand that
the tax should be reduced, on the ground that it was a
burden to both bank and community; on the other hand,
it was proposed to augment it, the argument being that
the banks were making a large profit on their circulation.[3]   As early as 1836 net income was proposed as the
basis of the tax.[4]   But in spite of these differences of
opinion on the merits of the tax and propriety of the
rate, the tax remained unaltered as long as state banks
existed.

Before the passage of the national bank law there were
in Massachusetts one hundred and eighty-one banks, with
an aggregate capital of $66,841,200, yielding, in 1863, a
tax of $646,728.   Not long after this tax had been im-
posed, it became the chief source of state revenue, enabling
Massachusetts for a long time to dispense with a state
levy on general property.   When the state was in need
of additional revenue, one of the expedients was to issue
more bank capital.   For the period 1831–1850 more than
three-fourths of the ordinary revenue of the state was
derived from this tax on banks, and in the decade 1851–

[1] Portland Bank *vs.* Apthorp; 12 Mass. 252.

[2] 1855, *Senate Document* 142, p. 142: 1855, *House Doc.* 293, p. 5.

[3] *Auditor's Report* for 1853, pp. 37-39, and the Reports of the Auditor
generally.

[4] Governor Everett's message, 1836, *House Doc.* 6, p. 18.

1860, when the state levy on property was again resorted to, more than one-half of the state revenues was still derived from this source. With the increased revenues demanded by the war and the introduction of the national bank system, the proportion of the total income derived from the bank tax declined, in the next five years, to about fifteen per cent. The revenue from it had reached its maximum in 1861 ($660,396) and declined rapidly after 1864. In 1865 the yield was only $284,975. In 1866 the revenue ceased with the disappearance of the state banks.[1]

III. *The Taxation of Insurance Companies and Savings Bank Deposits.*—The bank tax was the only important special business tax imposed on corporations. Domestic insurance companies, except stock companies, which were taxed on their shares, were exempt throughout the period before the war. Foreign insurance companies were subjected to a retaliatory tax as early as 1832.[2] The law of that year is notable as the prototype of the so-called "reciprocal acts" in other states. Agents for companies from states which taxed Massachusetts insurance companies were subjected to a tax of one-half of one per cent on the amount insured by them. In 1851 one per cent on the amount insured was imposed on fire and marine insurance companies of other states[3] and in 1852 one-half of one per cent was imposed on the amount insured by foreign life insurance companies.[4] The purpose of these two taxes was to replace the

---

[1] *Report of the Treasurer and Receiver-General* for 1864, p. 11; for 1865, p. 10; 1866, *Sen. Doc.* 3, p. 15.

[2] 1832, c. 140, §§ 1-2. *R. S.*, c. 37, § 45. *Cf.* Seligman, *Essays in Taxation*, p. 151. For earlier proposals to tax insurance companies see 1829, *House Doc.* 5 and 11.

[3] 1851, c. 331, § 7.   [4] 1852, c. 311, § 9.

revenue lost by the repeal of the auction tax.[1]   In 1854
these two provisions, the revenue from which had been
insignificant, were repealed.[2]   In 1856 all life insurance
companies were required to pay one cent for every
thousand dollars of insurance for the valuation of their
policies.   This, however, was a fee rather than a tax.   At
the same time the retaliatory taxation of foreign companies was restored; they were made liable to any taxes,
fines, and penalties to which Massachusetts companies
were subjected by the state of their origin.   Since that
date a similar provision has always formed part of the insurance law.   Insurance companies from foreign countries were by the same act taxed one per cent on all their
premiums and assessments.[3]   The policy of the state with
reference to insurance companies was obviously not directed to revenue.

Savings banks were not taxed directly.   Their deposits were, of course, taxable to the owners under the
general property tax.   As the growing accumulations
held by the savings banks aroused the assessors' attention, the attempt was made to secure the fuller taxation of
deposits through returns from the officers of the savings
banks to the assessors.   Not to discourage saving, however, the officers of the banks were required to make returns only of owners having deposits of five hundred
dollars or more.[4]   Local assessors might require returns
also for depositors with sums in excess of two hundred
dollars to their credit.   With the various exemptions
allowed by law to individuals and societies, and the many
forms of evasion readily available, only a very small part

[1] 1852, *House Doc.* 193, p. 2.   [2] 1854, c. 453, § 44.
[3] 1856, c. 252, § 47.   *G. S.*, c. 58, § 370.
[4] *G. S.*, c. 57, §§ 150, 152.

of the total deposits was taxed. So while deposits in 1860 amounted to $43,972,537 and in 1861 to $45,016,470, the amount taxed was little over one fifth, $8,847,588 in 1860, and $9,655,796 in 1861. In the taxation of savings bank deposits, as in the taxation of shares, the defect lay in attempting to reach the numerous owners instead of stopping the tax at its source.

For the period preceding the war, corporate property was thus taxed under the general property tax. Except for real estate and machinery the tax was assessed to the individual owners of the shares and collected from them. The results were a lack of uniformity and consequent injustice in the taxation of such property, and its escape in a large measure. There had however developed one important form of corporation tax as a special business tax. This tax was assessed directly on the banks by the state treasurer. The simplicity and efficiency of this form of tax administration suggested the adoption of a similar mode of administration in taxing all corporations. Likewise the need for revenue dictated the imposition of business taxes on corporate activity that had been exempt before the war.

CHAPTER II

TAXATION OF CORPORATIONS FROM THE CIVIL WAR TO THE PRESENT TIME

THE impelling motive for the reconstruction of the Massachusetts system of taxing corporations came from the need for more revenue created by the Civil War. While an average of one and a quarter millions of dollars had sufficed for the state's ordinary wants for the years 1856–1860, an average of four millions was needed in the next five years. The state levy on general property after reaching its highest point, three-quarters of a million dollars in 1857, had declined to an average of less than $300,000 for 1859–1861, and the expectation was that it would soon be abandoned. But in 1862 the state tax rose to a million and three-quarters, in each of the next two years the sum was doubled, and in 1865 $5,000,000 was imposed. At the same time, the introduction of the national banking system deprived the state of what had been its most productive source of income, the bank tax.

Taxes levied for local purposes increased at the same time. While in 1857 and 1858,[1] about six and a half million dollars in property taxes had sufficed for local needs; in 1861 there was imposed $7,300,000; in 1862 $6,800,000; in 1863 $8,200,000, and in 1865 $12,000,000. Thus in five years the local taxes had increased seventy-

---

[1] *Address of Governor Banks*, 1859, *Sen. Doc.* i, pp. xvi, xxvii.

five per cent. Instead of diminishing thereafter, the debts incurred during this period to avoid too heavy taxation and the expansion of municipal activity, led to constantly growing taxes. Expenditures and taxation did not return to the standards obtaining before the war. The taxes on general property, with which there is always levied in Massachusetts also a tax on polls, had, in a period of five years, doubled for the state as a whole (1861, $7,600,000; 1865, $16,800,000). Local and state needs demanded, with equal urgency, new sources of income.

I. *The Corporation Taxes.*—Attention was now turned to the taxation of corporations. In the first place, the endeavor was to create new sources of income, and to this end forms of corporate activity previously untaxed, or but inadequately taxed, were subjected to special business taxes. In the second place, measures were taken to reach more effectively the intangible corporate property taxed under the general property tax. For this purpose a centralized administration, a state machinery seeking to collect the tax at the source, was created. Avoiding the hampering restrictions of the general property tax, the legislature imposed excise taxes, and the Court upheld them by a very liberal interpretation of the clause in the constitution relating to the excise power.

This movement to tax corporations more adequately found its first expression in the imposition of a tax on savings banks and fire and marine insurance companies in 1862. The tax on savings banks yielded the next year over $400,000, where under the general property tax scarcely a fourth would have been collected. The tax on insurance companies yielded $88,000 in 1863, and $128,-000 in 1864, where, before, the revenue had been a trifle. In 1864 the general corporation tax, a tax on all corporations having a capital stock divided into shares, private business, financial, and public-service corporations alike, was adopted. Under this tax $100,000,000 was reached in 1864, where only $70,000,000 had been taxed in 1861. In the same year a special tax was levied on mining companies. In 1868 and 1871 the taxation of corporate shares at the source was adopted for banks.

Thus during the sixties, under pressure of the demands for revenue created by the Civil War, the Massachusetts system of taxing corporations was evolved. In the seventies, trust companies, as they were chartered, were taxed under the general corporation tax and their trust funds were added to the list of property taxed directly to corporations. In 1880, life insurance was subjected to taxation. Not till the late nineties was there any new development in the system that had grown up. Revenue and administrative efficiency had been the prime requisites in the sixties, and these demands showed themselves in the increased number of forms of corporate activity taxed and in the centralized administration created.

In the late nineties a new movement set in, a movement to disintegrate the general corporation tax, under which the greatest number of corporations are taxed, into a variety of special business taxes, adapted in the method of assessment as well as in that of distributing the proceeds to the nature of the industries subjected to taxation. In 1897 and 1898 this showed itself in additions to the law taxing street railways and in a change in the method of distributing the proceeds of the tax levied upon these companies. Still more is this tendency manifest in the revision of the general law taxing corporations in 1903, which distinguished for purposes of taxation business corporations from public service and financial corporations.

II. *Legal Basis of Corporation Taxes.*—In order to escape the limitations imposed by the general property tax, the legislature had recourse to its authority to impose excises. The constitution authorizes the General Court " to impose and levy reasonable duties and excises, upon any produce, goods, wares, merchandise, and commodities whatsoever, brought into, produced, manufactured, or being within the same." [1] This power had already been invoked in the bank tax levied in 1812. The Court then held that the term " commodity " embraced everything which may be a subject of taxation and signified " convenience, privilege, profits and gains, as well as goods and wares." There had been levied, at the time when the constitution was adopted, taxes on auctioneers, attorneys, tavern-keepers and retailers of spirituous liquors, and the court held that the tax on banks was analogous to these taxes on trades. [2] The question whether the business was carried on by a corporation or individual was not involved in the court decision. A point raised was whether the fact that the banks had been chartered without any stipulation as to taxation did not exempt them and this was decided in the negative. The tax, then, was upheld as a tax, not on the privilege of corporate existence, but on the privilege of carrying on the business of banking.

In the same case the court defined the limitations imposed on the excise power. Excise taxes must be equal,

[1] Pt. ii, c. i, art. iv.

[2] 12 Mass. 252. Referring to these earlier business taxes, the court said, " It is a commodity, convenience, or privilege, which the legislature by a contemporaneous construction of the constitution assumed a right to sell at a reasonable price and by a parity of reason it may impose the same condition upon every other employment or handicraft." See also 11 Met. 135, in which the term " franchise " is used.

that is, they must operate upon all persons who exercise the employment taxed. The advantage in resorting to the excise power lay in the greater latitude allowed in imposing excise taxes, as contrasted with the rigid requirements of the general property tax. Excises could be adapted both in rate and in administration to the particular conditions of the industry in question. This was impossible under the general property tax, under which a valuation of property and a uniform rate on all classes of property were required. Moreover intangible personal property had to be assessed to the owner at his residence. This had given opportunity for much evasion in the taxation of shares and deposits in savings banks. Furthermore federal securities, which became important at the time of the Civil War, were exempt, and corporations would have been free from the tax on investments of this class. It was progressively more difficult under the general property tax to reach much more than tangible property. The theoretical and practical inadequacy of the general property tax therefore commended the use of the excise power to the legislature.[1]

The first of the corporation taxes imposed after the beginning of the war, that on savings banks, was upheld, like the original bank tax, as a business tax. The Court decided that it was "an excise or duty on the privilege or franchise of the corporation." In its decision it said, "It is the extent to which the corporation has exercised the franchise conferred on it by law, of receiving deposits, during a certain period, that is made the basis on which to estimate the sum which is to be paid for the enjoyment of the privilege."[2]   In two subsequent cases the

[1] *Cf.* Seligman, *Essays in Taxation*, pp. 180–192, particularly pp. 186–187, 191–192.

[2] 5 Allen 428, and particularly p. 433; 12 Allen 312; 6 Wallace 611.

franchise was similarly held to mean the right to exercise a particular business. In another case involving the savings bank tax the Court said "commodity is a general term and includes the privilege and convenience of transacting a particular business, and upon persons carrying on such business, it has never been questioned that the legislature may levy an excise or provide that a license must be obtained in order to transact it."[1] Similarly the tax on life insurance companies was upheld as an excise on the franchise or function of receiving, investing, and managing the money of numerous policyholders.[2]

In the above instances, however, the businesses taxed were carried on by corporations. When it became desirable to reach through corporations corporate property that had been taxed to individual shareholders, the tax on these corporations was likewise assessed as a franchise tax. Here there was no longer any identity of corporate organization with the entire branch of business. The tax was not a special business tax, for no attempt was made to apply it to individuals or firms engaged in the same pursuits. What constituted the franchise taxed is not clear from the court's decision :

It is the capital stock considered as a franchise embracing the whole corporate organization, with all its rights and privileges, of which the shares are constituent fractional parts, that form the subject matter on which the tax or assessment is imposed . . . . . the actual value of the shares taken in the aggregate at the time of assessing the tax would be likely to show with approximate accuracy the actual existing value of the rights, privileges and benefits conferred by the franchise.

Identifying the tax on the corporation with the former

[1] 123 Mass. 495.   [2] 133 Mass. 161.

tax on corporate shares, the court concludes: "It is a tax based on the incorporeal right of holding shares in a corporation, and participating in the benefits of the franchise, estimated at its market value, whether assessed to the corporation on the aggregate of the value or to each stockholder on the market value of the separate shares."[1]

The corporations taxed by the law upheld in this decision were not only those engaged in public-service or financial enterprise, dependent on special charter, but also ordinary business corporations. The only characteristic common to all was the corporate form of organization. The franchise would therefore seem to mean no more than the right to exist and to carry on business as a corporation. Nevertheless, in the case of the tax imposed on foreign mining corporations, the court pronounced unfounded "the supposition that the existence and organization of the corporation, the functions and capacities with which it is endowed by the law creating it, are alone what constitute the franchise or "commodity," which is the subject of the tax.[2] It continues:

It is not merely the creation of corporate functions and privileges, or the conferring of rights and franchises by the legislature which entitles the state to tax the possessor of such privileges and rights. The exercise of powers and privileges, and even of occupations without special powers or privileges, may be equally subjected to such taxation under the constitutional authority to impose and levy reasonable duties and excises.[3]

Here the court would seem to have gone back to the view maintained in the original bank tax decision which it cites.

[1] 12 Allen 298; 6 Wallace 632.
[2] 99 Mass. 148.   [3] *Ibid.*, p. 152.

The decision just cited marks, however, the extreme attitude taken by the court. When the legislature attempted to tax, in the same manner as corporations, a class of business organizations which had sprung up to evade the corporation tax, "copartnerships and associations in which the beneficial interest is held in shares, assignable without the consent of the other associates,"[1] the court declared the act unconstitutional.[2] It held that while corporate franchises granted by the government, or foreign franchises which may by comity be exercised in the state, are subject to taxation, "the right to levy excises upon franchises has never been extended further than to corporate franchises specially granted by the government or enjoyed and exercised by its permission." These associations, enjoying no corporate or special privileges, could not be taxed. Here we see a reaction in the attitude of the court toward the excise tax, the decision condemning some of the utterances of the court in the

---

[1] 1878, c. 275, § 1.

[2] 134 Mass. 419. Indicative of the sentiment of the court is the following utterance: "If this tax can be upheld, it seems to us that the necessary result will be that the Legislature has the power to select any business, occupation or calling carried on, or any natural right enjoyed under the protection of our laws and impose upon it at its will a special tax or excise. This would be extending the meaning of the word 'commodities' beyond any reasonable limits. Its effect would be to break down the limitations which the constitution intends to impose upon the power of the Legislature, for the purpose of securing the end that all sums necessary for the defense or support of the government should as far as practicable be raised by taxation of the people."

See also Minot *vs.* Winthrop, 162 Mass. 121 *et seq.*, which reviews this case and comes to the conclusion that "The language of the constitution of Massachusetts in general may well be held to authorize the laying of excises upon all such gainful employments and privileges as are created or may be regulated by law, and commonly have been considered legitimate subjects of taxation in other states and countries." See also 190 Mass. 110.

early bank tax case, and in the case in which the excise on foreign mining corporations had been upheld, cases in which no special privileges were required as prerequisite for taxation under the excise power.

As a result of this decision and of some later ones, we may conclude that the franchise means either corporate organization or the right to conduct a business enjoying special privileges or requiring special regulation. The meaning given to the term commodity or franchise has been modified according to the exigencies of the time. Its original significance seems to have been no more than the right to engage in an industry which the government sees fit to tax. As corporations came to be subjected either to special taxes or to a special mode of taxation for the purposes of revenue or administration, corporate franchise was interpreted to mean the right to carry on a particular business regulated by the state, as that of savings banks or insurance companies, or the mere right to exist and carry on business in general, as a corporation.

III. *Administration of the Corporation Taxes—The Tax Commissioner.*—The introduction of corporation taxes involved the creation of an additional administrative department, that of the tax commissioner. When the tax on insurance companies and savings banks was imposed, the enforcement of it was entrusted to the treasurer. With the enactment of the general corporation tax in 1864, the treasurer and auditor were jointly made tax commissioners.[1] In 1865 the treasurer was designated tax commissioner[2] and authorized to appoint a deputy. To the latter was assigned the administration

[1] 1864, c. 208, § 5.
[2] 1865, c. 283, § 12; *Revised Laws*, c. 14, §§ 4, 35, 37 and c. 12, § 93.

of the general corporation tax. His duties in this connection are to transmit to the local tax assessors lists of
the corporations subject to taxation, to receive from the
assessors and from the corporations returns required for
determining the tax rate and for assessing the tax on
their franchise. On the basis of these returns he assesses
the tax on the corporations and apportions the revenue
to the state and the municipalities. He has also
duties connected with the bank tax.[1] From the treasurer's department there were transferred to the department of the tax commissioner the insurance taxes, in
1873, and the savings bank tax, in 1890, and the enforcement of the tax on life insurance companies had been assigned to him in 1880. The administration of all the
corporation taxes is therefore in his care.[2] In 1890 the
office of tax commissioner was separated from that of
treasurer and made an independent department.[3]

The closer interrelation of state and local taxation produced by the general corporation tax led to the imposition of additional duties on the tax commissioner, connected with the administration of the general property
tax. The effect has been to introduce a tendency toward
centralization in the entire tax system of Massachusetts.[4]
The growth of the corporation taxes, together with the
other duties of the tax commissioner, have made his department the most important in the fiscal administration
of the state. At the same time, the character of the

---

[1] 1873, c. 315, §§ 5–8; *R. L.*, c. 14, §§ 12, 13.

[2] 1873, c. 141, § 7; 1880, c. 227, § 2; 1890, c. 160, § 4; *R. L.*, c. 14,
§§ 20, 32.

[3] 1890, c. 160; *R. L.*, c. 14, § 1.

[4] *Cf. Report of the Commissioners relating to Taxation*, Boston, 1875,
p. 79 *et seq.*, and *Report of the Special Joint Committee on Taxation*,
1907, *House Document* 1090, pp.18–23.

Massachusetts system of taxing corporations, resting as it does on the market value of corporate stocks and on returns from local assessors and corporations, makes possible a simple, cheap, and, at the same time, effective machinery in both the assessment and collection of the corporation taxes.

IV. *Fiscal Importance.*—From these preliminary historical and legal considerations we pass to a survey of the importance of corporation taxes in their fiscal aspect, their place in the revenue system, and in their economic aspect, their relation to industrial life. Considering first the fiscal aspect, the importance of the corporation taxes becomes evident on comparing the revenue from these taxes with the revenue from other sources in state and local finance. In this connection it is of interest to note also the amount and the kind of property reached by the corporation taxes, as compared with that assessed under the general property tax.

A. In the development of the Massachusetts system of taxing corporations the segregation of state and local sources of revenue has not been the sole motive. The creation of sources of state income independent of the general property tax was the motive for the taxes on insurance companies and savings banks. Hence these are the most important corporation taxes the yield of which is reserved exclusively for state use. On the other hand, the taxes on general corporations and banks were imposed primarily to secure the fuller taxation of

---

[1] The corporation taxes as assessed by the tax commissioner amounted to $8,484,151 in 1905 and $7,673,598 in 1904. The cost of the tax commissioner's department, as reported by the auditor, exclusive of expenses connected with the general property tax is less than $30,000. The cost of assessing the corporation taxes is, therefore, little more than one-third of one per cent.

corporations. The revenue from these taxes, which are the most productive, is shared by the state with the municipalities; the local bodies receiving between two-thirds and three-fourths of the total yield. The principle by which the division is determined is the residence of the shareholders. The state retains so much of the tax as corresponds to the part of the stocks of Massachusetts corporations which is owned outside of the state; the rest of the revenue is distributed among the cities and towns in which the shareholders reside. This method of distribution was followed exclusively up to 1898, when it was abandoned in the apportionment of the tax on street railways. There is now a demand for the adoption of a better system in distributing the tax on other corporations.

A very great proportion of the total yield of corporation taxes has always become part of the local revenue. This proportion increases with the growing productivity of the general corporation tax, and the amount received by cities and towns from the general corporation and bank taxes exceeds the amount accruing to the state from all corporation taxes. Thus in 1905 the state received from the tax on savings banks, and the insurance taxes and licenses, $2,709,000, and from the taxes on banks and other corporations, $1,713,000, in all, $4,422,-000. The municipalities on the other hand received from the taxes on banks and corporations $5,464,000.[1]

B. In the revenue system of the state the corporation

[1] For the data see *Auditor's Report* for 1905. Only the corporation taxes which became part of the general revenue have been included; the taxes for maintaining the railroad and gas commissions and various fees have not been considered. The amount of the bank tax retained by cities and towns (as reported by the Tax Commissioner) has been added to the amount returned to the cities and towns by the state.

taxes may be regarded as the chief source. The other important elements contributing to the support of the state are the annual levy on general property, the state's share of the receipts from liquor licenses, and the inheritance tax. For the period 1901–1905 these contributed forty-five per cent of the state's receipts available for general purposes. The corporation taxes, on the other hand, yielded fifty per cent. The remaining revenue is derived from state institutions and a variety of fees and licenses. The relative proportion of the various sources of revenue is shown in the following table:

CHIEF SOURCES OF THE REVENUE AVAILABLE FOR GENERAL PURPOSES.[1]

(Average for 1901–1905.)

	Amount.	Per cent.
Total	$8,315,000	100.0
State tax on general property	2,450,000	29.4
General corporation tax (retained by state)	1,300,000	15.6
Bank tax (retained by state)	382,000	4.5
Tax on savings banks[2]	1,661,000	19.8
Insurance taxes and licenses	757,000	9.1
Collateral inheritance tax	539,000	6.4
Liquor licenses	813,000	9.7

Likewise for a longer period, corporations have furnished about one-half of the state revenue, as appears from the following table:[3]

[1] For data see *Auditor's Report* for 1905, p. 11. In addition a special tax is assessed on railroads and street railways for the maintenance of the railroad commission ($50,282), on gas and electric companies for the maintenance of the gas and electric light commission ($32,920), and a variety of fees on corporations, domestic ($66,373), and foreign ($8,-810. There were in 1905 in all over $150,000.

[2] Including the Massachusetts Hospital Life Insurance Company.

[3] This table is constructed from data in the auditors' reports. In the first column the total revenue has been determined by deducting loans and interest on loans guaranteed by the state. It is only roughly approximate.

CHIEF SOURCES OF STATE REVENUE, 1871-1900.

(Averages for five year periods in thousands of dollars.)

	(1871–1875.)	(1876–1880.)	(1881–1885.)	(1886–1890.)	(1891–1895.)	(1896–1900.)
Total revenue	$4,938	$4,228	$4,932	$5,282	$6,215	$7,333
General property tax	2,150	1,260	1,700	1,950	1,850	1,600
Corporation taxes	314	281	648	664	898	1,184
Bank tax	222	171	447	427	454	403
Savings bank tax[1]	1,516	1,763	1,034	979	1,176	1,356
Insurance taxes[2]	199	200	283	343	445	555
Liquor licenses	......	138	216	357	554	750
Collateral inheritance tax	......	......	......	......	......	440
Per cent of total revenue.	100.0	100.0	100.0	100.0	100.0	100.0
All corporation taxes	45.0	56.9	48.6	43.5	47.6	47.4
General property tax	43.5	29.8	34.4	36.9	29.7	21.8
Liquor licenses	......	3.2	4.3	6.7	8.9	10.2
Collateral inheritance tax	......	......	......	......	......	6.0

For municipal finance corporation taxes have far less importance than for state revenue. Here the chief source of income has always been the general property tax[3] as appears from these figures for 1904:[4]

	Total Corporate Receipts.[5]	General Property Tax.[6]		Corporation Taxes.	
		Amount.	Per Cent.	Amount.	Per Cent.
Boston	$25,070	$17,659	70.4	$1,509	6.0
Worcester	2,963	1,938	65.4	258	8.7
Fall River	1,810	1,269	70.1	57	3.1
Cambridge	2,434	1,693	69.5	167	6.8
Lowell	1,893	1,312	69.3	102	5.3
Lynn	1,456	907	62.3	61	4.1
New Bedford.	1,494	1,035	69.2	104	6.9
Springfield	1,713	1,036	60.4	147	8.5
Lawrence	1,002	647	64.5	33	3.2
Somerville	1,398	1,007	72.0	72	5.1

[1] Including tax on Massachusetts Hospital Life Insurance Company.

[2] Including insurance licenses.

[3] Thus, in the period 1880-1900 Boston derived between sixty-five and seventy per cent of her total income (except that from loans) from the general property tax, and only between five and seven per cent from the corporation and bank taxes. See Boston Statistics Department, *Special Publications*, no. 5, tables II, VII, and table facing p. 20.

[4] Bureau of Census, Bull. 50, *Statistics of Cities*, tables 10 and 25.

[5] Exclusive of loans.   [6] Including poll tax.

Of the total receipts of the larger cities between three and nine per cent is derived from the taxes on banks and on corporations, as against sixty to seventy per cent from the tax on general property. These percentages for 1904 do not differ much from those for previous years.

The disparity in the proportions of the total revenue accruing from corporations to different cities is due to the present mode of distribution, which is based on the residence of the owners of the shares. The residential towns in which the shares are owned to a very large extent, are especially benefited by this system. Some of these receive from the corporation taxes very large sums enabling them to enjoy a low rate of tax on general property.' In addition to these taxes distributed by the state, the municipalities receive from street railways a commutation tax, devoted to the maintenance of the streets, amounting in 1905 to about $380,000.

The average amount, distributed to cities and towns, for 1901–1905 from the taxes on general corporations and banks was $4,595,000 or a sum equal to nearly nine per cent of the average amount of taxes levied in the state on general property ($52,979,000) for these years. This sum is far in excess of the state tax on general

---

[1] Thus for 1905:

	Property tax.	Received from bank and corporation taxes.
Brookline	$1,103,503	$273,088
Milton	282,328	73,811
Manchester	92,309	51,903
Webster	56,254	41,094
Weston	52,269	30,252
Nahant	50,365	38,439

property, which averaged $2,450,000 for the same period, and would permit Massachusetts not only to defray all state expenditures without resort to the property tax, but also to reduce the county taxes by more than one-half.[1] Were therefore considerations of revenue alone to be followed, the corporation taxes would enable Massachusetts not only to attain to a segregation of state and local sources of revenue, but also to approximate this ideal for county taxes. Municipalities would thus be left almost undisturbed in the exploitation of the general property tax.

C. The importance of the corporation taxes may be seen further from the amount and kind of property reached through corporation taxes, as compared with the property actually reached by the general property tax. Here it is to be noted that while personal property assessed by the local assessors increases but slowly, and while tangible personalty constitutes the greater portion of the total,[2] the personal property taxed through corporations has augmented more rapidly, and is intangible in character. In 1865 the value of corporate shares, in excess of the value of real estate and machinery which is taxed locally, was equal in amount to twenty per cent of the personalty assessed in the state under the general property tax. This "corporate excess" was equal to forty-eight per cent in 1905. Adding thereto the value of bank shares, the sum is equal to sixty per cent of the personalty assessed by the local assessors. If we include savings bank deposits, trust funds, and the net value of life insurance policies, the personal property taxed through

---

[1] For 1901–1905 the average is $3,394,000.

[2] See *Report of the Tax Commission,* 1897, pp. 44–49.

corporations is far in excess of the personal property taxed locally, as may be seen from the following table:[1]

	1895.	1900.	1905.
General property (total valuation)......	$2,542,348	$2,961,119	$3,312,255
Personal property[2]............................	539,159	610,789	679,769
Corporate excess.............................	242,125	315,335	343,374
Bank shares	112,608	95,300	86,077
Deposits in savings banks (taxable)[3]	249,986	295,206	362,440
Net value of life insurance policies ...	64,841	87,758	122,789
Total taxed through corporations......	669,560	793,599	914,680

Moreover, while the personal property taxed by local assessors in the forty years since 1865 has increased less than one hundred per cent, and since 1885 less than fifty per cent, the " corporate excess " or value of the shares of corporations over and above their real estate and machinery, has increased three hundred per cent, and since 1885 one hundred and fifty per cent. Similarly the taxable savings bank deposits were in 1905 six times as great

---

[1] For the earlier period the information is not available in as detailed form. The data for the table above and the following table are taken from the reports of the treasurer, and of the tax commissioner, and from the *Aggregates of Polls, Property, Taxes*, etc., compiled by the secretary of the commonwealth.

	Total valuation of general property.	Personal property.	Non-resident bank shares.	Corporate excess.	Savings bank deposits.*
1865......	991,841	386,079		79,941	59,936
1870......	1,417,127	516,089		92,063	135,745
1875......	1,840,732	529,701	31,113	84,213	237,848
1880......	1,584,756	473,596	28,289	105,983	208,825
1885......	1,782,349	494,355	28,529	138,755	165,403
1890......	2,154,134	553,996	30,006	212,777	216,296

*The taxable deposits after 1880 represent little more than one-half of the total deposits.

[2] Exclusive of bank shares.

[3] Including deposits in trust companies.

as in 1865, and double what they were in 1885. The net value of life insurance policies is more than three times as great as in 1880, when the tax was first imposed. Corporation taxes are thus obviously a better means of reaching intangible property than a tax on the individual owners of intangible personalty.

Comparing the amount yielded by corporation taxes with the total yield of the general property tax, the relative proportions have not varied greatly since 1871. The yield of the corporation taxes has been equal to about one-sixth of the revenue from the general property tax. As compared, however, with the revenue from the tax on personal property, the amount yielded by the corporations has increased very much more rapidly, being equal to more than sixty-five per cent of the personal property tax as levied by the local assessors in 1880 and more than eighty-five per cent thereof in 1905. The burden of the ever-increasing local expenditures continues, however, to fall on general property. The general property tax therefore still remains the chief source of revenue in the state, and particularly the tax on real estate, which alone contributes over three-fifths of the total tax revenue, state and local. This is shown in the following table of the chief taxes, assessed in the state:[1]

[1] The taxes on corporations, in more detail, are as follows:

	1871.	1880.	1890.	1900.	1905.
	(In thousands of dollars.)				
Corporations (general)	$1,536	$1,642	$3,212	$5,156	$5,921
Banks (less amount refunded)..	1,277	1,197	1,476	1,311	1,296
Savings banks	1,179	1,616	1,064	1,470	1,809
Insurance companies	116	127	203	317	446
Life insurance companies	......	186	120	219	306

The data are taken from the reports of the tax commissioner, of the treasurer, and from the *Aggregates of Polls, Property, Taxes*, etc.

	1871.	1880.	1890.	1900.	1905.
	(In thousands of dollars.)				
Total corporation taxes	$4,108	$4,768	$6,075	$8,473	$9,778
Total general property taxes	22,063	24,755	31,503	47,914	57,476
Amount on personal property	7,192	7,059	7,657	9,894	11,744
Liquor licenses	......	......	......	3,219	3,361
Collateral inheritance tax	......	......	......	397	694

VI. *Economic Importance.*—The significance of the corporation taxes becomes clear, when we note the relation of the corporate form of organization to industry in its different branches. First of all there is to be observed the vast-growth of public-service corporations since the Civil War, and particularly since electricity came to be utilized in urban transportation, and as a source of light and power. Electricity has led to a remarkable development in street railways; the extension of the use of the telephone has made very rapid strides; gas, and particularly electric companies, have multiplied and extended their activity. Public-service industries— a field generally restricted to corporate enterprise—have thus greatly expanded.

Financial institutions, another field of corporate activity, have similarly experienced a rapid growth. The trust companies have added their activities to those of the banks, and savings banks have been amassing ever greater sums of deposits. Insurance, in all its forms, has enlarged its scope. But while financial and public-service enterprise assumed the form of corporate organization from the outset, this period has witnessed a rapid growth in the adoption of this form of industrial organization for ordinary business enterprise.' While this has

[1] In 1875 Massachusetts corporations engaged in manufacturing were credited with almost as great a capital as private firms. They were employing about 40 per cent of the labor force, and produced about 35

been particularly marked in the case of manufacturing companies; since the middle of the nineties it has become increasingly frequent for commercial concerns also to incorporate. The new business corporation law adopted in 1903 has moreover greatly facilitated the adoption of corporate organization for general business. Corporate organization is the dominant form in industry. The taxation of corporations is therefore likely more and more to become the chief method of taxing business.

The importance of the taxes on corporations to the public is further indicated by the character of the corporations which contribute most of the revenue. This is shown in the following table:[1]

		(In thousands of dollars.)
Public Service Corporations		3,585
Municipal utility.		
Street railway	979	
Telephone and telegraph	486	
Gas and electric	321	
Water...................	8	
Railroads	1,708	
Steamboat..	80	
Other Corporations for Private Gain		4,089
Manufacturing and mercantile.		
Domestic	1,685	
Foreign	48	
Financial.		
Banks (net)	1,296	
Trust	478	
Insurance	580	
Corporations for Savings		2,133
Savings banks............	1,809	
Life insurance	323	

per cent of the output. *Cf. Ninth Annual Report of the Mass. Bureau of Statistics of Labor* (1878), pp. 87, 88.

For 1905, in the thirty-two leading industries, the output of which was equal in value to about three-fourths of the total manufactures, corporations employed 73 per cent of the wage-earners, and are credited with 71 per cent of the total output. *Cf. Bureau of the Census, Bulletin 53, Census of Manufactures*, 1905, *Massachusetts*, p. 28.

[1] Data taken from *Auditor's Report* for 1905.

Of the total, aggregating in 1905 about ten million dollars, public service corporations paid more than one-third, or three and a half millions. Municipal utility companies—street railway, telephone and telegraph, gas and electric companies, furnished one-half of this sum; the other half came from railroad and steamboat companies. A large part of the taxes is thus paid by corporations which minister directly to the public as consumers.

Corporate activity undertaken primarily for private gain contributed even a larger sum, or more than four millions. Here the bulk of the taxes is paid by financial corporations. Manufacturing and trading companies supplied one and three-quarter million dollars. Banks and trust companies furnished a similar sum, and insurance companies added one-half million dollars. Taxes levied on private business thus yield less than one-half of the imposts on corporations.

Corporate enterprise pursued primarily for its general social utility—savings institutions and life insurance companies — contributed more than two million dollars. Savings banks paid one million eight hundred thousand dollars, and life insurance companies three hundred thousand dollars. A very considerable proportion of the total taxes on corporations are, therefore, levied on savings or income.

CHAPTER III

The General Corporation Tax

In discussing the Massachusetts corporation taxes, we shall begin with the most important, the general corporation tax. Under the general corporation tax there were taxed, and with the modifications introduced in 1903 there are still taxed, three groups of corporations: ordinary business corporations, public-service corporations, and trust and stock insurance companies. It will be our purpose to discuss first the general aspects of this corporation tax, and then to consider the tax in connection with the larger problem of the taxation of these groups of corporate industries.

1. *General Features* —Dissatisfaction with the taxation of shares in corporations had led as early as 1860 to a proposal that the tax on corporate shares be collected by state officers directly from the corporations, and that the revenue be distributed among the municipalities by the same officials.[1] It was not, however, until 1864 that a law for this purpose was placed on the statute book. The chief defects of the taxation of shares under the general property tax had been administrative. Decentralized administration had involved a lack of uniformity in the valuation of the shares of the same corporation in different towns, had given ample opportunity for evasion, and had allowed escape from taxation to the shares of

---

[1] 1860, *House Documents*, no. 111, 153.

non-residents. Even a cumbersome system of correspondence between assessors and corporations could not en-
sure complete taxation. A special tax on the shares of
non-residents had been declared unconstitutional. The
acts of 1864 and 1865[1] sought therefore to attain the
uniform valuation and the complete taxation of shares by
substituting, on the administrative side, a central state
agency for the local assessors and by imposing the tax
directly on the corporation, instead of seeking to reach
the stockholder.

In instituting this reform the practices of the general
property tax were adhered to as closely as possible in determining the basis of the tax, the rate to be imposed,
and the method to be followed in distributing the proceeds. The new corporation tax was, in form, only the
previous tax on shareholders centralized in administration. The change involved, however, an important departure in principle, for it really meant the taxation of
corporations in place of individuals.

The law of 1865 made provision for the taxation of all
Massachusetts corporations, except banks of issue and deposit, organized for the purpose of business or profit, and
having a capital stock divided into shares. Banks were
excluded because they were under federal charter.[2] The
only other corporations excluded were companies organized to engage in mining out of the state,[3] and later to

---

[1] 1864, c. 208; 1865, c. 283.

[2] The act of 1864 did not exclude banks, but in 1865 the banks had
assumed national charter; furthermore, the act of 1864 applied to corporations " located in " the state as well as to those organized under Massachusetts laws. 1864, c. 208, § 2. The guarantee capital of mutual fire
and marine insurance companies was at the recommendation of the tax
commissioner made taxable. 1872, c. 375, §§ 11, 12; see *Tax Commissioner's Reports* for 1869, p. 14, and for the following years.

[3] 1864, c. 208, §§ 10, 11; 1865, c. 283, §§ 8, 9, 10.

engage in the building of railroads and telegraphs in foreign countries.[1] These were excepted because of the peculiar conditions of their business activity and taxed differently. On the other hand, foreign telegraph companies were expressly made taxable under this general law in 1865,[2] foreign telephone companies in 1885,[3] foreign street railway companies in 1898,[4] and finally foreign railroad companies.[5] Other foreign corporations except those engaged in mining, were left to the general property tax. The taxation of foreign corporations did not become a problem until the nineties. The general corporation tax thus applies to public-service corporations, whether domestic or foreign, except gas and electric companies, express companies, and special service car companies. Otherwise it applies only to domestic corporations.[6]

The basis of the tax on corporations, as of the former tax on shares, is the market value of the capital stock, after deducting the value of the real estate and machinery subject to local taxation. The excess of the value of the shares, over the value of the property taxed by the local assessors, is taken as the basis in order to avoid the double taxation of corporate property. Corporations are required to furnish to the tax commissioner returns of the amount of their capital stock, the par and the market value of their shares on May first, and to present

[1] 1879, c. 274, § 6.   [2] 1865, c. 283, § 7.

[3] 1885, c. 238.

[4] 1898, c. 417, at the recommendation of the Railroad Commissioners. See *Report of the Railroad Commissioners* for 1897, p. 124.

[5] *Revised Laws*, c. 14, § 37, and more clearly 1906, c. 463, pt. ii, §§ 211, 212.

[6] The law taxing corporations is contained in the *Revised Laws*, c. 14 (1902). Subsequent changes are referred to specifically.

a statement describing their works and structures,[1] their real estate and machinery, taxed locally in and out of the state.[2] Interstate railroad and telegraph companies, and interstate street railways,[3] are required to make returns of their capital stock, as above, of the total length of their lines and the length of their lines in Massachusetts, and of so much of their property as is taxed locally within the state. Telephone companies report, in place of the length of line, the number of telephones. Since 1902 corporations other than street railways are required to make returns also of equipment situated in the streets.

The tax commissioner, on the basis of the returns submitted, or of other information, ascertains the market value of the shares of the corporation, and estimates the fair cash value of all the shares constituting the capital stock. This sum is regarded as the "true value of the corporate franchise." For the larger corporations there is of course no difficulty in discovering the value of the shares from current market quotations. For smaller corporations the tax commissioner is guided by their statement of assets. He is empowered to require corporations to submit books, and to examine officers of corporations for the purpose of determining the value of the franchise.

From the "true value" of the "corporate franchise,"

---

[1] In 1902 (c. 342), corporations other than street railways were made taxable locally for underground conduits, wires and pipes in the street and they were required to make returns to the tax commissioner of these items. He now makes deductions for this kind of property, taxed *in situ*, in determining the corporate excess.

[2] This deduction for merchandise and machinery situated outside of the state appears first in the act of 1865, having been introduced at the recommendation of the tax commissioners; see *Report* in 1865 *House Doc.* 126, p. 7.

[3] 1898, c. 417.

the tax commissioner deducts for ordinary corporations the value of the real estate and machinery taxed locally, under the general property tax, in Massachusetts or outside of the state.[1] For the purpose of these deductions he may be guided by the valuation placed upon this property by the local assessors, or he may revise their assessment. The excess of the value of the shares over the value of the property taxed locally,—the real estate and machinery,—is termed the " corporate excess." This forms the basis on which the corporation tax, as assessed by the state, is levied. The corporate excess for interstate railroad, telegraph and street railway companies, is determined by taking an amount of the capital stock at its market value corresponding to that proportion of the total line which is located in Massachusetts.[2] For telephone companies the number of telephones is the more accurate measure of the proportion of the capital on which the tax is based. For these corporations only the property assessed locally in Massachusetts is deducted from the market value of the shares.[3]

The rate of the tax on corporate excess has been made to approximate roughly the average rate of taxation in the state on all property. In 1864 the rate was fixed by the legislature at one and one-sixth per cent, approximately the average rate on property at that time. In 1865 the law made provision for a rate that fluctuates

---

[1] By court decision mortgages on Massachusetts real estate, which are regarded as an interest in real estate, are also to be deducted. *Cf.* 137 Mass. 80.

[2] The act of 1864, c. 208, §§ 3, 6, made the cost of the road the basis, but this simpler method was adopted the next year.

[3] The Supreme Court of the United States upheld this feature in the case of the Western Union Telegraph Company. 125 U. S. 530; 141 U. S. 40.

with the average rate on property. This rate is determined by the tax commissioner by apportioning the taxes on property, exclusive of polls, levied or to be levied in the cities and towns of the state in the given year, on the total valuation of property for the state in the preceding year. The valuation of the preceding year is taken for convenience. The resulting rate, however, is not, strictly speaking, the average rate of the tax on property. In 1906 the rate for all corporations except railroad, railway, and electric railroad corporations, was made the average of the annual rates thus determined for the three years preceding the assessment.[1] On the advice of the tax commissioner the Joint Special Committee on Taxation of 1907, in its report, recommended that this rate be made uniform for all corporations. The change prevents large fluctuations of the rate from year to year, and brings the rate on corporate excess nearer the average rate of the tax on property.

The tax levied by the commissioner is paid to the state treasurer. The proceeds are distributed according to the rules of the general property tax, that is, according to the residence of the shareholders in the corporations assessed. For this purpose corporations must furnish the tax commissioner with returns of the names and residences of their shareholders and of the number

---

[1] 1906, c. 271, §§ 9, 12. This exception of the railroad and street railway companies seems to have been due to the oversight of this act in codifying the railroad laws. *Report of the Joint Special Committee on Taxation*, 1907, pp. 8, 42. The significance of the change may be seen from the fact that for 1905 the rate on corporate excess would have been $16.51, whereas the actual rate was $17.25, and the average rate for property was $16.83. Under the law as it stood up to 1906, as long as the valuation of general property was increasing from year to year, the corporation tax rate, owing to the way in which it was determined, would be greater than the average rate on general property.

of shares held by them. The amount of the tax corresponding to the value of the shares held by non-residents of the state remains in the commonwealth treasury, the rest is credited to the cities and towns and offset against the sums due to the state from the property tax and bank tax. The principle that personalty follows the owner is still observed, the only departure being in the case of the tax on street railways. Here the mileage of the street railways forms the basis for distributing the proceeds among the municipalities.[1]

The Act of 1865, as thus described, remained in force without any modifications of consequence to 1903, when extensive alterations were introduced in the tax as it applies to business corporations. For public service and financial corporations, which yield by far the larger part of the revenue, it is still unchanged. Briefly, therefore, the features of the taxation of corporations are: (1) the local taxation of real estate and machinery by the assessors of the cities and towns; (2) the taxation by the state of the value of the capital stock in excess of this tangible property; (3) the collection of this tax on corporate excess directly from the corporation by the state; (4) the division of the yield from the tax between the municipalities and the state, according as the shares of the corporation are owned in their jurisdiction or outside of the state. As already noted, exception is made in the distribution of so much of the tax as is levied on street railways. The entire amount is in this instance returned to the cities and towns. Except, as noted before, in the case of most public-service corporations, the general corporation tax applies only to domestic corporations. Under it no effort is made to tax bonds.

[1] 1898, c. 578, § 4.

These are left for assessment under the general property tax.

II. *Taxation under the General Property Tax.*—The corporation tax has for its background the general property tax. It seeks to tax corporations indirectly for property that is not reached by the general property tax. Without entering upon the general problems of the property tax, we shall summarize here so much of the law as has relation to our subject, adhering closely to the text of the statutes.[1]

All property, real and personal, situated within the commonwealth, and all personal property of the inhabitants wherever situated, is subject to taxation, unless expressly exempted by law. Real estate is defined so as to include not only all land, but also all buildings and other things erected on or affixed to the land. It is assessed to the owner or person in possession in the city or town in which the estate is situated. With regard to real estate, it is to be observed that in the case of railroads[2] and other public-service corporations, land acquired by eminent domain, and buildings situated on it, are exempt. Otherwise corporations and individuals are taxable alike for real estate.

Personal estate includes goods, chattels, money and effects, wherever they are, ships and vessels at home and abroad, money at interest, and other debts due the person to be taxed more than he is indebted or pays interest for. From the taxation of debts due loans on a mortgage of real estate are, however, in effect, exempt. Personal property further includes public stocks and securities, bonds of railroads and street railways, stocks in turnpikes, bridges, and moneyed corporations within or

---

[1] *Revised Laws*, c. 12, §§ 3-5, 15, 23.   [2] 4 Met. 564.

without the state. The shares in corporations taxable under this clause are, however, only shares in foreign corporations. Incomes under certain limitations are also taxable as personal estate. There are a variety of exemptions, but these do not concern us here.

All personal estate, within or without the state, is assessed to the owner in the city or town in which he is an inhabitant. The exceptions to this rule that personalty follows the owner are numerous and important. In general, tangible property is taxable where it is located. Thus goods, wares, merchandise and other stock in trade, and stock employed in the business of manufacturing or of the mechanic arts, in cities or towns, other than those in which the owners reside, are taxed where the owners have their place of business, whether such property is there or not at the time of assessment. Machinery employed in manufactures is taxed where it is situated. Likewise personal property leased for profit is taxed where it is situated. Personal property held by guardians is taxable where the beneficiary resides, unless the beneficiary lives outside of the state. Then it is taxed where the guardian has his residence. In 1902 underground conduits and wires and pipes laid in the public streets by any corporation, except street railways, were made taxable to the corporation *in situ*.[1] So far as tangible property used in business is concerned, it is made taxable where it is located.

One of the features to be noted in the taxation of personal property in Massachusetts is that tangible property is taxed without any deduction for debt. Intangible property may be offset by debt, but even here the intangible property from which indebtedness may be de-

[1] C. 342.

ducted is limited to money at interest and debts due. A decision of the court[1] held, in 1884, that railway bonds and corporation bonds generally were to be classed under debts due, from which debts owed might be deducted, but the legislature[2] soon after explicitly added railroad and street railway bonds to the class of personal property from which debts may not be deducted.

In the taxation of personal estate, corporations and individuals are treated alike only with regard to machinery. To both it is assessed according to its situs. Other personal property is not locally taxable to domestic corporations. The practice of assessing tangible property,[3] in general, according to its location had been established early. The reason why this practice was not extended to merchandise of corporations is probably the fact that in 1832, when the systematic taxation of corporate shares was adopted, and later in 1864, when the general corporation law was enacted, commercial corporations had not yet assumed importance. With the recent growth of mercantile corporations the demand is that stock in trade be taxed to corporations, like machinery, that is, according to its location. Under the law as it stands, tangible personalty, in general, is taxable to individuals directly; as regards domestic corporations, however, personal property other than machinery can be reached only through the tax on their capital stock. Individuals are, moreover, liable to taxation for personal estate situated outside of Massachusetts, but with the present methods of assessment, the assessors are not likely to discover such property.

[1] 137 Mass. III.   [2] 1888, c. 363.
[3] *Cf.* e. g., 1830, c. 86, § 4, 5. *Revised Statutes*, c. 7, § 10. For machinery, see 1837, c. 86. *General Statutes*, c. 11, § 12.

Foreign corporations, other than public-service corporations expressly included under the general corporation tax, are reached through the general property tax. Since 1903 a slight excise tax is also levied. With regard to taxation they are treated like non-residents, and, by court decisions, they can be assessed only for property that is made liable to taxation regardless of the residence of the owner. This means, in effect, that they are liable only for tangible property used in business.

While Massachusetts seeks to avoid the double taxation of the property of her domestic corporations, the law provides for assessing shares in foreign corporations at their full value. Whether the corporations, the property of which is represented by the shares, have been taxed elsewhere or not, is not considered. Under the general property tax bonds in both foreign and domestic corporations are also taxable.

The assessment of personal property in Massachusetts is based chiefly on estimate, and not on sworn returns. This applies to both tangible and intangible property. The estimate of the assessors, guided by visible evidences of property and prosperity, has been found satisfactory in practice, particularly as regards the taxation of merchandise.[1] The tax on machinery is, however, felt to be a burden.[2] Machinery and stock in trade together constitute probably more than one-half of the total personal property taxed in the state.[3] From the method of assessment pursued, it appears that the taxation of business in Massachusetts means practically the lenient taxa-

---

[1] *Report of the Tax Commission*, 1897, pp. 53–57. See also *Report of the Joint Special Committee on Taxation*, 1907, p. 45.

[2] *Report of the Tax Commission*, 1897, p. 56.

[3] *Ibid.*, pp. 46–48, 50, 263.

tion of tangible property employed in business. The taxation of intangible property has proved a failure in Massachusetts as elsewhere.[1]

III. *The Working of the General Corporation Tax.* —We return to the corporation tax and consider its operation. The tax on corporations gave general satisfaction from the outset,[2] and for twenty-five years there was scarcely any complaint. The tax commissioners in their report, after the law had been in operation one year, showed that two hundred and eighty-two municipalities had benefited by the change, some very greatly, that only thirteen had suffered, and these only slightly. For the towns and cities a very large amount of taxable personalty, at least $6,000,000, had been added to the list by the more efficient mode of taxation. At the same time a considerable income had been made available for the state, where none had existed before, by retaining in the state treasury the tax on shares of non-residents.[3] The tax did not have the effect of discouraging corporate enterprise, for there was an increase both in the number and in the capitalization of corporations.[4]

The value of the corporate shares taxed rose gradually, although it varied from year to year, as the value of corporate securities fluctuated with industrial conditions. In the forty years since 1865 the value of the shares taxed has increased more than fivefold, and the income accruing both to state and municipalities has grown like-

[1] *Report of the Tax Commission*, 1897, p. 67.

[2] Message of Governor Andrews, Jan. 6, 1865, in *Mass. Acts and Resolves* for 1865, pp. 734-735.

[3] See *Report of the Tax Commissioners* in 1865, *House Doc.* 126, pp. 5, 6, 13, and appendix, and also the *Report of the Tax Commissioner* for 1865, pp. 44, 45, 48.

[4] See *Report of the Tax Commissioner* for 1869, pp. 11, 14.

wise, until, in 1905 and 1906, it was four times the amount in 1865. The tax rate throughout averaged about one and a half per cent. The distribution of the tax as between municipalities and state has given about one-fourth of the revenue to the state and three-fourths to the various towns and cities. Details may be gathered from the following table:

THE GENERAL CORPORATION TAX, 1865–1906.[1]

(In thousands of dollars.)

	Value of Shares.	Real Estate and Machinery.	Corporate Excess.	Tax Assessed on Corporate Excess.	Distributed to Cities and Towns.	Retained by State.	Tax Rate.
1865..............	$146,790	70,184	79,941	1,421	1,060	361	17.56
1870..............	199,041	106,977	92,063	1,425	1,077	360	15.44
1875..............	239,848	170,240	84,213	1,236	915	321	14.68
1880..............	251,565	160,675	105,983	1,626	1,204	422	15.35
1885..	309,502	194,649	138,755	1,961	1,484	476	14.14
1890..............	460,022	263,478	212,777	3,157	2,360	797	14.84
1895..............	545,869	325,817	243,361	3,642	2,642	999	14.95
1900..............	641,664	349,356	315,731	5,108	3,761	1,346	16.14
1905..............	784,241	480,525	343,878	5,856	4,470	1,386	17.25
1906..............	851,120	524,678	373,995	6,103	4,535	1,568	16.87

A tax commission sitting in 1874, after the tax had

---

[1] As assessed by the tax commissioner, from whose reports the figures are taken.

been in operation ten years, expressed its satisfaction with the corporation tax in the following language:[1]

We regard it as the most valuable contribution to fiscal science, and other states have already copied its methods. After ten years' trial it receives the approval not only of assessors, but of stockholders and corporations. It is direct as to corporations, and hence challenges attention and investigation. It is indirect to the stockholder, and upon him the pressure is not irritating. . . . Its method of assessment and collection is simple, sure, and inexpensive.

The criticism of this commission related to the imperfect method of valuing the corporate franchise on the basis of stock only, whereby corporations with bonds escaped with a lighter tax. It also called attention to the tendency of local assessors to place a high valuation on locally taxed property, thus depriving the state, and the municipalities, in which the shareholders resided, of a portion of the tax due to them under the law.[2] It did not, however, propose any definite changes.

[1] *Report of the Commissioners.........relating to Taxation and Exemption*, Boston, 1875, pp. 124-125.

[2] This was particularly an abuse at this period. The effect of the corporation tax had been to secure a fuller valuation of the real estate and machinery belonging to corporations, the result was that an ever increasing proportion of the property of corporations was taxed locally, leaving less and less to be taxed through the tax on corporate excess. In 1865, locally taxed property represented 48 per cent of the value of the shares, in 1870, 53 per cent, and in 1876, 73 per cent. While after 1872, owing to the depression, the value of shares did not advance or even declined, local assessors for a time continued to increase their valuation of real estate and machinery. But this high valuation on real estate and machinery as compared with the value of the shares was in part at least due to the greater responsiveness of the market value of shares than of the valuation of tangible property to business depression. After the return of prosperity, the value of the shares rose rapidly again, the proportion taxed locally fell to 55 per cent in 1881. See *Report of*

Twenty years later, another tax commission again gave its approbation to the Massachusetts system of taxing corporations. "As a whole, this part of our system is an excellent example of the method of taxing corporations at the source, and of refraining from any dealings with the individual holder of corporate securities—a method admitted on all hands to be the simplest, most efficient, and most equitable in the taxation of corporate property."[1] Describing the operation of this tax and the similar bank tax it says:

The real estate and machinery are assessed locally ; doubtless not with perfect equality and justice, but probably as carefully as would be possible under any system. The corporate excess is taxed at a uniform rate by the state. The taxes are regular and certain. They are heavy, and they yield a large revenue. . . . Yet little complaint is heard regarding these taxes,—a signal proof that the taxpayers accomodate themselves, if not with ease, at least without serious complaint to burdens which are steady, regular, predictable, and for which in consequence they are able to make calculations and adjust their affairs.[2]

Beginning in 1890, however, there set in an agitation for the modification of the corporation tax in two directions. The prominence into which electricity had brought street railways, gave rise to the demand for a special franchise tax on street railways and on public-

the Tax Commissioner for 1867, p. 7; for 1876, p. 9; *Report of the Tax Commission*, 1875, p. 127; *Report of the Tax Commission*, 1897, p. 55. For the period up to 1895 real estate and machinery to about 60 per cent of the value of the shares were taxed by the local assessors. This percentage declined to 52 per cent in 1903. In consequence of the changes in the law in 1903, the percentage rose again in 1904 to 57 per cent.

[1] *Report of the Commission on Taxation*, Boston, 1897, p. 70.

[2] *Ibid.*, pp. 68-69.

service corporations generally.   The contention was that such companies enjoy a special opportunity for profit, created by the community.   They ought therefore to be taxed differently from ordinary business enterprises, and assessed also for the exceptional privilege conferred on them.   This agitation led to a provision in 1898 levying an additional tax on street railways, when dividends exceed eight per cent.[1]   The demand now is for an extension of this principle more widely to the field of public-service corporations.[2]

The second criticism related to the mode of distributing the proceeds of the tax, and was connected with the demand for a special franchise tax.   The end sought in both cases was a compensation from public-service corporations to the municipalities from which they derived their earnings.   In the case of street railways the distribution of the tax was altered to meet this demand.   The old rule that personalty follows the owner was abrogated; the proceeds were assigned to the cities and towns in which these companies operate.[3]   The dissatisfaction with the present mode of distributing the tax is wider and the demand is for more extensive modification.

While there was complaint of the general corporation tax as a tax on public-service corporations, a phenomenon which became prominent in the nineties led to dissatisfaction with its operation as a tax on business corporations, namely, the competition of corporations under foreign charters with domestic corporations in the state. Under certain conditions foreign corporations engaged in manufacturing and trading in Massachusetts enjoyed an advantage over domestic corporations, as the Massachusetts tax laws stood.   Modifications of the law which

---

[1] 1898, c. 578, § 3.   [2] See chapter v.   [3] 1898, c. 578, § 4.

would place the two classes of corporations on a footing of equality as regards taxation were demanded.[1] The law of 1903, regulating business corporations, provided, therefore, that business corporations should be treated differently and in effect more leniently than the other corporations in matters of taxation. The general corporation tax in its original form thus became a tax on public-service corporations and on trust companies and stock insurance companies.

IV. *Significance for Various Classes of Corporations.* —It becomes then important to consider the corporations taxed under the general corporation tax according to the kinds of business in which they are engaged. The simple and uniform method of taxing all corporations alike seems destined soon to give way to a number of taxes, adapted to the particular conditions of the special business to be taxed. In the absence of statistics indicating the relative importance of corporations in different classes of business, from the point of view of the value of their capital, we indicate here their fiscal importance:

RELATIVE IMPORTANCE OF CORPORATIONS.[2]

(In thousands of dollars.)

	I. Total Tax on Corporate Excess.	II. Public-Service.	III. Financial.	IV. Business.	V. Per cent of Total.		
					II.	III.	IV.
1871	1,461	827	180	453	56.	12.	31.
1875	1,235	689	136	409	55.	11.	33.
1880	1,603	826	179	597	51.	11.	37.
1885	1,934	1,082	165	686	55.	8.	35.
1890	3,077	1,905	206	965	62..	6.	31.
1893	3,651	2,250	260	1,140	61.	7.	31.
1905	5,814	3,585	543	1,686	61.	9.	29.

For the period beginning with 1871, for which statistics

[1] See chapter iv.   [2] The figures are taken from the auditor's reports.

are available, from fifty to sixty per cent of the tax has come from public-service corporations, the proportion of the tax paid by public-service corporations increasing notably since 1885. Of the remainder, about ten per cent is contributed by trust companies and insurance companies having a capital stock, so that only about thirty per cent of the tax arises from manufacturing and trading corporations.

The reason for this disproportion in the amount of tax paid respectively by these different groups of corporations is to be found in the different methods of taxing these corporations locally. Public-service corporations have a great part of their property exempt from local taxation, and this is true of almost all property in the case of financial institutions. On the other hand, manufacturing corporations are apt to have most of their capital invested in real estate and machinery locally taxable. Hence the greater corporate excess of the former class of corporations, and the greater justification for the complaint of the injustice resulting from the distribution of the tax.[1]

V. *Criticism.*—The general problems with regard to the tax on corporations are concerned with (1) the propriety of the present method of assessing the corporation tax on the value of the capital stock alone, (2) the significance of the tax on corporate excess for different corporations, and (3) the distribution of the tax.

The effect of calculating the value of the corporate franchise for taxation on stock alone is obviously to give an advantage to corporations with property represented by indebtedness. If corporate property were all represented by stock, the market value of the corporation

[1] See chapter v.

might be presumed to stand for a capitalization of net earnings. The tax might then be regarded as equivalent to a tax on net earnings. Where, however, there is indebtedness, the capital stock at its market value stands for only a part of the net earnings capitalized; property and earnings represented by indebtedness, therefore, escape. The method employed in Massachusetts would thus tend to put a premium on corporations issuing bonds rather than stock.

Whether the desire to escape taxation be a reason or not, there has been a marked increase in the bond issues of street railways and railroads, as may be seen from the following table,[1] indicating the percentage of funded debt to the capital stock at par:

	Street Railways.	Railroads.
1870	20	22
1880	36	51
1890	40	65
1895	79	66
1905	79	66

The amount exempted is not so great as is indicated by this table, at least, not for the successful corporations, the value of whose stocks is far above par, whereas bonds are closer to par; but it is none the less considerable. The result of taxing corporations on capital stock only is, therefore, to exempt corporations from taxation on a large part of their productive capital. Originally this basis for taxation was less objectionable in Massachusetts than elsewhere, for her railroads had been built very largely by the issue of stocks rather than of bonds. But there has since been a large addition to the funded debt of such corporations, and in the case of other public-service

[1] For data see *Reports of the Railroad Commissioners.*

corporations bonds represent a very large proportion of the property. Capital stock is consequently an inadequate basis for taxation.

Moreover, inasmuch as the proportion of bonds to capital stock is not a constant one for all corporations in the same class, or for all groups of corporations, the consequence must be inequality both as between corporations in similar enterprises, and as between different groups of corporations. In theory bonds are, of course, taxable to the owner, but aside from the fact that a considerable portion is owned outside of the state, very little personal property of this character is reached by the local assessors. The tax commission of 1875 recognized the evil arising from this inadequate basis for taxation, but suggested no remedy.[1] Although, more recently, there has been a growing demand that this inequality be remedied, and that corporations be taxed on the market value of both stocks and bonds,[2] no change has yet been made in the law.

Another criticism of the market value of the stocks as a basis for taxation is the fluctuating character of prices for securities.[3] From the fiscal point of view the fluctuating character of the basis of the tax, even where quotations can be obtained easily, means that the yield of such taxes cannot be accurately foretold. Moreover, as stocks decline in value in times of depression, a smaller tax is imposed on corporations, and a greater share of the public revenues must then be derived from the general property tax. But, in practice, this is not serious,

---

[1] *Report*, pp. 127–128, 174.

[2] *Report of the Joint Special Committee on Taxation*, 1907, pp. 31 *et seq.*

[3] See *Report of Tax Commissioner* for 1904, p. 21.

inasmuch as the formation of new corporations tends, even in years of depression, to add to the total value of corporate shares. The use of quotations for the first of May,[1] or as near that date as possible, would seem to be open to criticism, but no fault has been found with this method of determining the value of the capital stock. On the other hand, this system, particularly in the case of the railroads and other public-service corporations, has the patent advantages of avoiding the necessity of an elaborate machinery for valuing corporate property and assessing corporation taxes.[2]

The market value of stocks can not, however, be used as the basis for all corporations. For the smaller companies, whose shares are not on the market, the difficulty of determining the proper valuation for taxation was noted by the tax commission of 1875.[3] Here, in the absence of market quotations, the tax commissioner naturally assumes the value of the corporation's capital stock to be the net assets.[4] To this extent the tax becomes a tax on property rather than on capitalized earnings, and is thus open to the objection against a tax which is assessed on property without considering its income-bearing character. Moreover, here too, as in the case of the larger corporations, the tax, whether assessed on the net assets or on the market value of stock, is levied on a valuation which does not take ac-

---

[1] See interview with the tax commissioner in *Report of the Ontario Commission on the Taxation of Railways*, p. 122.

[2] See *Report of the Joint Special Committee on Taxation*, 1907, pp. 31, 32.

[3] *Report*, p. 127. See also *Report of the Tax Commission* of 1897, pp. 16, 69.

[4] *Ibid.* See also *Report of the Committee on Corporation Laws*, 1903, p. 40, and *Report of Tax Commissioner* for 1905, pp. 24, 25.

count of debts. The result is that corporations enjoy
the privilege, not accorded to individuals and firms, of
deducting their debts not only from intangible property,
but also from tangible property. By the creation of indebtedness it is, moreover, possible to lighten or even to
escape taxation completely, a possibility of which the
corporations avail themselves.[1] There is, therefore,
room for inequality and evasion.

The significance of the tax on corporate excess thus
differs for various corporations, both public-service and
ordinary business corporations, according to the amount
of indebtedness. In the case of the latter class of corporations the character of the property, in which the
capital is invested, is also of importance. Where corporations have the major part of their capital invested in
real estate and machinery taxed locally, there is often no
corporate excess on which to levy the tax.[2] Such corporations are thus exempted from any tax on other
tangible and intangible property which they may possess. The earlier tax commission, whose ideal was the
full taxation of all property, found fault with this phase
of the operation of the tax.[3] This feature has since met
with favor, because it reduces the tax burden of manufacturing corporations, which are otherwise laboring
under adverse circumstances in Massachusetts and are
complaining of the weight of taxation.[4] In the business
corporation law of 1903 no change was therefore introduced in this phase of the tax.

[1] *Report of the Committee on Corporation Laws*, p. 56.

[2] *Report of the Committee on Corporation Laws*, p. 45; see also chapter
iv, p. 81, note 1.

[3] *Report of the Tax Commission*, 1875, p. 127.

[4] *Report of the Tax Commission*, 1897, pp. 56–57. It urged the exemption of machinery as soon as the financial situation of the state and
local bodies would permit the change.

This phase of the tax on corporations operates, at least in theory, in favor of the corporation as compared with the individual or the firm; the latter being taxable not only for all tangible property, but also for intangible property in excess of debts. The advantage is however offset, in part at least, by the laxer[1] method of taxing even tangible personalty under the general property tax. For private corporations whose capital is invested in merchandise the advantage is still greater, since such merchandise is not taxed locally, and since indebtedness can be the more readily offset against merchandise than against machinery.

On the other hand, private corporations whose assets consisted largely in intangible property such as patent rights, or whose earning capacity relatively to their tangible property was great, were taxed on these elements through the tax on the corporate excess, where individuals or firms would not be assessed on such assets under the general property tax. Such corporations early sought to avoid this tax by forming voluntary associations with shares transferable like those of corporations.[2] These the court held could not be taxed as corporations.[3] In the nineties, foreign charters were adopted whereby it became possible to escape taxation on all property except that of a tangible nature. In order to retain such corporations under a Massachusetts charter, it was therefore necessary to reduce the tax on "corporate excess," and this was done in the business corporation law of 1903. These considerations, affecting primarily business corporations, are rather of an historical interest, casting some

---

[1] *Report of the Tax Commission,* 1897, pp. 53 *et seq.*

[2] *Report of Tax Commissioner* for 1870, p. 14.

[3] 1878, c. 275; 134 Mass. 419.

light on the operation of the tax for this class of corporations up to 1904, when the tax laws as applied to business corporations were extensively modified by the act of the preceding year.

Leaving for later chapters the working of the tax in the case of the different groups of corporations, we may observe here that neither for public-service corporations nor for private corporations is the general corporation tax a uniform tax on capitalized earnings. Its merits lie rather in its superiority to the general property tax in administrative efficiency than in its approximation to the more ideal system of taxing net earnings directly or indirectly.

VI. *Distribution of the Tax.*—In the division of the proceeds of the tax on corporate excess the state has throughout this period, received about twenty-five per cent of the total tax.[1] The share of the tax accruing to the state differs for private corporations and public-service corporations. The stocks of the latter naturally enjoy a wider market and hence about thirty per cent of the tax on these corporations, representing the percentage of stocks owned outside of Massachusetts, is retained in the state treasury   Only about twenty per cent of the tax on business corporations goes to the state.[2]

The remainder of the tax, distributed to the cities and towns according to the residence of the shareholders, tends to an increasing extent to go to the residential centers, and away from the industrial towns. As early

---

[1] See table, p. 57.

[2] See data in *Report of the Committee on Corporation Laws*, p. 67. The amount of the tax on railroads, retained in 1906 by the state, is equivalent to 37 per cent of the total tax ($1,597,063). See *Report of the Joint Special Committee on Taxation*, 1907, p. 132; also 1901 *House Doc.* 1342.

as 1870, sixteen cities and towns received seventy per cent of the tax distributed, Boston alone receiving nearly one-half of the amount going to the municipalities. In 1880 sixteen cities and towns again received about the same amount; Boston's share had, however, declined to one-third of the total. On the other hand the proportion allotted to such towns as Brookline, Milton, Nahant and Newton had increased.[1] For 1896 the tax commission found that Boston with twenty per cent of the population received more than thirty-three per cent of the total amount distributed ($856,000). Boston received almost as much as the other thirty-one cities ($922,000) although these had more than double Boston's population. The share of Boston was also greater than that of all the towns ($807,000), although they had one and a half times the population of the metropolis. Eighteen selected towns with a population of 62,000 received nearly a third of the tax going to all the towns with twenty times their population.[2] Since then, this tendency has continued, and the receipts from the tax on corporations, other than street railways, are concentrated even to a greater extent in a few favored localities.[3]

[1] For data see the tax commissioners' reports.

[2] See *Report of Tax Commission*, 1897, p. 67, and appendix, table G. While the per capita rate of the corporation tax distributed was for the state $1.03, it was $1.72 for Boston, $1.08 for the cities taken as a whole ; 93 cents for all the towns, but $5.31 for the selected residential towns, and 59 cents for the remainder. The per capita rate for Brookline was $7.74, for Milton $7.94, Hopedale $10.64, Manchester $11.29, Nahant $22.68; the per capita rate for Brockton was 22 cents, for Everett 8 cents, Fall River 19 cents, Lynn 41 cents, Lawrence 24 cents, Lowell 82 cents, and Cambridge 84 cents.

[3] The share of Boston has declined since 1896, only 30 per cent of $3,421,000 distributed going to this city in 1905. The thirty-two cities outside of Boston in 1905 received only 35 per cent, making the tax apportioned to the cities 65 per cent. Nearly one-half of the total tax

In order to realize the injustice of the distribution of the tax, we need only remember that about sixty per cent of it arises from public-service corporations, and and about one-third from railroads alone. In the case of railroads and of public-service corporations generally, their property is to a very great extent exempt from assessment by the local authorities. The existing method of distribution therefore often means that the towns and cities from which the corporations derive their earnings and in which their property is situated, receive but a small return. In the case of financial and trading corporations, sometimes no tax at all is paid to the place where the corporation carries on its business.

In connection with the public-service corporations, therefore, where local property is largely exempt, and a considerable proportion of the shares are owned outside of the state, a demand for a change in the method of distributing the revenue from the tax first arose. Plans have been offered advocating that the state retain the entire tax and defray with the part now distributed the expenses of the counties,[1] or retain a greater part of it, so as to avoid a heavy state levy on general property.[2]

goes to Boston, Brookline, Newton, Springfield, and Worcester. The towns having very much less population than the cities outside of Boston nevertheless receive about as great a proportion of the tax as these cities. Here, however, twenty-four received more (20 per cent) than the remaining *297* (15 per cent). In other words, while Boston receives a smaller percentage of the tax, the share going to fashionable residential suburbs is far greater in 1905 than in 1896.

Illustrative of the inequalities occasioned by the present distribution is the fact that while Brockton receives $29,700, Everett $4,100, Fall River $28,800, Lawrence $18,600, Brookline receives $218,000, Milton $68,100, Manchester $47,100, Webster $40,100, and Nahant $30,800. See data in appendix to *Report of the Tax Commissioner* for 1905.

[1] *Report of the Tax Commission*, 1897, p. 116.

[2] *Report of the Joint Special Committee on Taxation* 1907, pp. 35 *et seq.*

Other proposals urge that the tax be distributed according to school attendance for the support of education,[1] or that an amount equal to a tax on the property exempted be returned to the localities where such property is situated, or that the distribution be according to population, gross receipts and the like.[2] So far a departure has been made in the distribution of the proceeds only for the tax on street railways. The entire amount received from such corporations is divided among the cities and towns served by these companies, the mileage of tracks being used as the basis for distribution. The result of this change has been a large gain to Boston and to industrial towns, and a loss to purely residential towns. To take extreme instances, under the changed system of distribution Methuen was to receive, for 1896, $2,337 where it had received, before, $5; Everett $10,085 where it had received $433. On the other hand, eighty-nine towns formerly receiving $25,800 were to receive nothing.[3] A similar result would follow from a change in distribution of the tax on railroads.[4]

The inequalities wrought by the general method of

[1] Cf. e. g., 1893, House Doc. 111.

[2] Cf. e. g., 1905, House Doc. 193, 194; 1906, House Doc. 550, and particularly 551.

[3] See Report of the Special Committee on the Relations of Cities and Towns and Street Railways, 1898, appendix, and also Report of the Rapid Transit Commission, 1892, pp. 116-119, and appendices, pp. 123, 280, 281.

[4] For 1906 Boston received about one-third ($341,000) of the railroad tax ($996,000) ; Cambridge, Lowell, Springfield, and Worcester together less than one-sixth, or less than the amount received by Brookline, Falmouth, Lexington, Manchester, Milton, Nahant, Newton, Swampscot, Webster and Weston. The rest of the state receives less than one-third. Such industrial towns as Lynn, Lawrence and Fall River receive but trifling amounts. See appendix to Report of the Special Joint Committee on Taxation, 1907.

distributing the tax are well summed up in the statement of the commission of 1897: "On the whole, the present method of distributing corporate excess seems to us to be based on a doubtful principle, and to work badly in practice." Speaking of its effects, the commission says: "It results in an arbitrary apportionment of large sums of money, with little visible regard to the real claims and needs of the several cities and towns."[1] The commission proposed to retain the entire tax on the corporate excess and to defray with it the county expenses, a plan involving an extension of state functions. The Joint Special Committee on Taxation of 1907, advocated, in view of the growing need of the state for revenue, a departure from the method of distributing the tax now in vogue, in two respects. They recommended in the first place that the state retain in the state treasury the tax accruing from railroads and telegraph and telephone companies—a change which would add to the state revenue, from the tax on railroads alone, nearly one million dollars. Furthermore, heeding the complaints of Boston and other cities, they urged that the tax on mercantile corporations be returned to the cities and towns in which their tangible property is located.[2]

The inequalities involved in the present distribution of the tax and the manifest injury wrought by it to the industrial centers, whose needs for revenue are greatest, raise the problem as to what is the proper principle of distribution. The principle that personalty follows the owner is inadequate, and has long been abandoned in Massachusetts in taxing most tangible personalty. It is doubly improper when the tax represents in a great measure tangible property, and even real estate, exempted

[1] *Report*, p. 71.   [2] *Report*, pp. 35–39, 45, 46.

from local taxation. The relation of the community to the corporate industry would seem to be a proper principle for distribution, and the limits of the community correlated with a corporate industry should be the confines within which the tax is expended.

In the case of public-service corporations, the community, state or municipality creates the field of activity and the occasion for carrying on the business, whether it creates a special opportunity for profit or not. In the case of municipal utility corporations, it would be proper on this principle to return the proceeds of the tax to the municipality. Where the activity of the corporation is inter-municipal, some basis of division must be devised that will measure the opportunity for business and profit created by each of the cities or towns served. Corporation receipts might be taken as a measure, or a rougher and more practicable guide might be selected. For street railways the length of track has been adopted and found satisfactory, though obviously it is not accurate. For gas companies, to the extent that they are not local, the length of pipe, for electric companies the length of wire, for telephone companies the number of instruments, would afford a ready basis for apportioning the proceeds of the tax. For the railroads and telegraph companies, and for other transportation agencies, like steamboats, the field of activity is wider and to a great degree coextensive with the entire state. Here it would seem proper that the receipts be distributed according to population, or preferably be retained by the state.

The problem in the case of private business corporations is of a different character. For manufacturing concerns the market often has no relation to the place of business. The relation of the corporation to the community assumes another form. The corporation adds to the population, and creates greater needs for revenue, to be expended for the education of the children of employees, and for local improvements. At the same time the activity of the corporation does not necessarily increase in proportion to the per capita wealth of the community, since the owners of the corporation often reside elsewhere. For trading corporations, the market is in a great measure local. Moreover, corporations unlike individuals do not pay taxes on their merchandise locally. On the other hand, business creates special expenditures, necessitating additional fire protection, care of streets and the like. For trading and manufacturing corporations the special cost to the community would justify retaining the tax in the locality in which the corporation conducts its business.

For purely financial institutions, such as insurance companies, trust companies, and banks, where the field of activity is complex and less definable, the proper policy would seem to be for the state to retain the tax, or to distribute it on the basis of population. The former policy is followed in the taxation of all financial institutions except stock insurance companies, trust companies and banks.[1]

Under a plan of distribution based on the relation of corporate activity to the community, the tax on some corporations can be made a source of state income and the tax on other corporations a source of local income. The present mode of distributing the tax on street rail-

[1] See also F. A. Wood in an article, entitled " Massachusetts Franchise Tax and Local Distribution," in *Municipal Affairs*, iv, pp. 124–128. He recommends the situs of property as a basis of distribution. "The corporation is the taxpayer, its taxable situs is where its business is carried on," p. 127. He would retain the tax on railroads in the treasury, because its " field of exploitation is the entire state."

ways is a step in this direction, and the special tax committee of 1907 would extend the application of this principle.

The separation of source to the extent of excluding the municipalities from the revenue yielded by the corporation taxes may not be altogether desirable in Massachusetts. The present corporation taxes yield a revenue largely in excess of the state's requirements. There would, therefore, be a need for the extension of state activity in order to absorb the excess revenue. Neither would it be satisfactory, in assigning the revenue from certain groups of corporations to the municipalities, to hand over some of the corporation taxes to local administration, for, with the complicated character of corporate activity, effective administration of corporation taxes is bound up with centralized state assessment and collection.

Briefly then, the advantages involved in the Massachusetts system of taxing corporations are the comparative simplicity and the effectiveness of the administration of the tax. The valuation of shares alone, instead of shares and indebtedness, results in inequality as between corporations, and opens the way for evasion. The distribution of the proceeds of the tax tends to concentrate the income in residential centers, and thereby deprives the industrial centers of a much needed revenue.[1]

[1] For the general system of taxing corporations in Massachusetts, the most important references are the *Reports of the Tax Commissions* of 1875 and 1897. The report of 1875 is particularly valuable for its account of the earlier history of the corporation taxes. The other references to public documents and to literature are given in the notes.

Prof. C. J. Bullock's essay, "The Taxation of Corporations in Massachusetts," in the *Quarterly Journal of Economics*, vol. xxi, pp. 181–246, appeared when this monograph was virtually completed. Summaries of the corporation tax system are found in the *Report of the*

The significance of the corporation taxes may best be seen when they are treated as part of the general taxation of corporations under the peculiar conditions surrounding particular groups of corporate industries. We turn therefore to the more detailed examination of the taxation of corporations, taking up first the taxation of private business corporations, then public-service corporations, and finally financial corporations.

Industrial Commission, vol. xi, pt. vii, pp. 14-19, and in the *Report of the Ontario Commission on Railway Taxation*, 1905, pp. 115-125.

CHAPTER IV

TAXATION OF BUSINESS CORPORATIONS

THE general corporation tax, like the earlier tax on shares, did not draw any distinction between general and special corporate franchises. The legislator, finding that the market value of stocks often exceeded the value of the tangible property of a corporation, proceeded to tax this corporate excess as the law termed it. A value in excess of property is of course not associated in industry exclusively with corporate organization. In the case of corporations, however, it is possible to discover this surplus more readily, and to reach it for taxation. The Massachusetts legislator did not stop to inquire whether it arose from a special privilege conferred by the government, or from business success, due to other causes. He was content to accept for all corporations the market value of the corporate stock as a test of ability to pay taxes. Hence all forms of corporate activity pursued for private gain, were taxed alike on their capital stock, and no exception was made for business corporations.

The general corporation tax, as we have seen, applied only to domestic business corporations. Foreign corporations were treated like non-residents, and taxed, in theory, even more leniently than individuals and firms. When, therefore, in the nineties, corporate organization came to be widely adopted, and states began to compete for the business of issuing charters, mercantile and manufacturing corporations were often afforded an opportunity to escape this tax on corporate excess by exchanging their Massachusetts charters for foreign charters.   To retain these corporations for Massachusetts it became necessary to reduce the tax, where it discriminated against domestic corporations.   The remedy adopted in 1903 was to tax these on little more than their tangible property.   The abandonment of capitalized earnings for tangible property is from the point of view of the theory of taxation a step backward.   The practical situation, created by interstate rivalry for the issue of charters, thus set at nought the theoretical considerations.

I. *Taxation of Business Corporations under the General Corporation Tax.*—By business corporations, to use the term of the law of 1903, are here meant corporations other than public-service or financial corporations, that is, companies engaged in enterprises requiring no special supervision or regulation by the government.[1]   Such corporations are comparable to individuals and firms, differing from the latter in the character of their organization, but not in the field of their activity.   When the general corporation tax was adopted, the business corporations taxed under it were for the most part manufacturing corporations.   In the nineties, however, trading concerns incorporated with increasing frequency. The effect of the new law, facilitating the organization of corporations, has been to stimulate further this tendency[2] of business to adopt corporate form.

Up to the nineties, domestic corporations occupied the field.[3]   The question then was, whether the mode of tax-

---

[1] 1903, c. 437, § 1, Corporations organized to engage in public-service or financial enterprise outside of Massachusetts are, however, included under the law of 1903.

[2] *Infra*, pp. 67, 68.

[3] In 1885 the tax commissioner reported that five hundred foreign cor-

ation was not more favorable to corporations than to individuals and firms. All were alike taxable locally on their real estate and machinery. Corporations were, however, taxable for their merchandise and intangible property only through the tax on their corporate excess, whereas individuals and firms were taxable locally for their tangible property and, in theory at least, also for credits and cash on hand. Moreover, corporations whether taxed on a market valuation or their stocks or on their net assets, enjoyed the privilege of offsetting tangible property by debts, a privilege not accorded to individuals or firms. When engaging in business outside of Massachusetts the corporation had a further advantage, in theory, over the individual in that it was not taxed for machinery situated outside of the state, whereas the individual was by law taxable for all personalty owned by him. So far as the law was concerned, the gain was for the most part on the side of the corporation. These advantages were, however, minimized by the fact that business property is assessed by the local assessors on an estimate,[1] whereas under the corporation tax, returns to the tax commissioner provide a more effective machinery for assessment.

The only corporations taxed more heavily than individuals or firms were corporations whose capital stock represented intangible property, such as patent rights, trade marks or good will, and very successful corporations, whose stocks were worth much in excess of the

porations having a usual place of business had filed certificates of organization as required by law. In 1890 the total number had risen to 1,454; in 1900 to 4,649; in 1903 to 6,321; in 1906 to 7,247. See *Reports of the Tax Commissioner*.

[1] *Report of Tax Commission*, 1897, pp. 53–56; *Report of the Joint Special Committee on Taxation*, 1907, p. 45.

value of their tangible property, that is, the corporations possessing the greatest taxpaying ability.   In order to escape this tax, businesses so situated **organized**, in some instances, as voluntary associations with shares like those of a corporation.   These could not be reached under the corporation tax.[1]

So long as Massachusetts corporations competed only with individuals and firms taxed by local assessors, there was no complaint of the corporation tax.   The difficulty arose when, in the nineties, it became more and more frequent for corporations to carry on their business in Massachusetts under foreign charter.   While the obstacles to corporate activity imposed by the Massachusetts corporation law were in part responsible for the situation, the burden of the Massachusetts corporation tax was held to be one of the chief causes, if not the chief cause, for the standstill of corporate activity under Massachusetts charters, and for the rapid increase in the number of foreign corporations doing business in the state.[2] From 1897 to 1901 there was scarcely any increase in the number of corporations annually chartered.   On the other hand the annual number of foreign corporations to file papers in order to do business in the state, which

[1] See also J. M. Hallowell, "The Corporation Franchise Tax," in *Review and Record*, Sept. 17, 1904 (reprint p. 7).

[2] *Cf. Report of the Committee on Corporation Laws*, 1903, p. 16.   See also Hallowell, *op. cit.*, p. 6, quoting Lucius Tuttle, President of the Boston and Maine Railroad, "There is an opinion prevalent among the business people of this state that something is wrong with our laws in that our very best industries conducted wholly in Massachusetts seem to think it is necessary to go to other states to get charters, and in some cases have surrendered charters taken in Massachusetts and replaced them with charters from other states. . . . . . .But after all, gentlemen, the main question is that of taxation.   You may remedy all your laws and wipe away all those to which I have referred, but if you don't touch the question of taxation, you might as well leave them all alone."

had been about as great as the number of Massachusetts incorporations in 1897, had doubled by 1901.[1]

To what extent might a corporation profit by a foreign charter? A foreign corporation was, under the law, liable to taxation only for tangible property which was made expressly taxable *in situ*, in effect, only real estate, machinery, and merchandise.[2] The shares indeed were taxable to the shareholder, if discovered, but the chance of discovery by local assessors was not a serious menace. Foreign corporations thus escaped taxes on all intangible property. To the extent then that intangible property formed the assets of a corporation, or in so far as the value of its shares was largely in excess of its tangible property locally taxable, its tax as a foreign corporation would be less than as a domestic corporation. The most successful corporations, accordingly, had much to gain from foreign charters.

The relative advantages of foreign and domestic corporations may be seen from the situation in 1901. Of the two thousand Massachusetts manufacturing and trading corporations, fifty per cent, having nearly two-thirds of the total capitalization, paid less in taxes than they would have paid as foreign corporations. They were taxed in the aggregate on a corporate excess of $46,054,-678, while they had merchandise to the value of $113,-654,957. As the value of their shares was less than the value of their tangible property by $67,600,279, they were exempt on sixty per cent of their merchandise, and their saving was more than a million dollars.[3]

[1] *Report of the Committee on Corporation Laws*, p. 20.

[2] *Revised Laws*, c. 13, § 23; 158 Mass. 461: 161 Mass. 326; *Report of the Committee on Corporation Laws*, p. 37; *Report of the Joint Special Committee on Taxation*, 1907, p. 50.

[3] Manufacturing and trading corporations with twenty-four per cent of the total capitalization of the business corporations, had a capital stock

On the other hand, nine hundred companies with one-third of the capitalization were taxed on a corporate excess greater than the value of their tangible property. While their tangible property untaxed locally amounted to $29,949,072, their corporate excess was $58,183,961; they paid therefore on intangible property amounting to $28,234,889. As foreign corporations they might have saved the tax on this sum, or nearly a half million dollars. The Massachusetts tax was thus prejudicial to some of its most successful corporations, the corporations whose capital stock had a market value in excess of tangible property, and to those companies whose investments did not take the form of tangible property. A smaller number of corporations neither gained nor lost by their Massachusetts charter.[1]

valued at less than their real estate and machinery, and, therefore, paid no corporation tax. Not being taxed on anything except real estate and machinery, these were taxed very much more lightly as domestic corporations, than they would have been as foreign corporations.

[1] The following tabulation of the calculations made by the committee on corporation laws indicates the relative advantages and disadvantages of foreign and domestic corporations for taxation in 1901. The tax rate assumed is for convenience $16.00, the tax rate for that year being $16.-18. *Cf. Report*, pp. 43-50.

(In thousands of dollars.)

MASS. CORPORATIONS.	Number.	Capitalization.	Corporate excess.	Value of Merchandise.	Corporate excess greater or less than the value of merchandise.	Per cent of		Gain or loss for taxation as foreign corporations.
						Capitalization.	Number.	
Total number..................	2,045	240,582	104,238	143,604	−39,365	100.	100.	−710
Corporations whose merchandise exceeds in value their corporate excess.............	1,024	152,819	46,054	113,654	−67,600	63.	50.	−1,081
Whose corporate excess is more than their merchandise.............	901	76,051	58,183	29,949	+28,234	32.	44.	+451
Whose corporate excess balances their merchandise.....	7	56						
With no corporate excess or merchandise......	103	11,656						

There were some other impediments to the activity of Massachusetts corporations under the general corporation tax. The tax law made holding companies impossible, for the shares of a holding company, even if these stood for the stocks of Massachusetts corporations already taxed, were again liable to taxation. Furthermore, corporations seeking to engage in business in several states were hampered by the fact that in taxing them for their franchise no deduction from the value of their shares was allowed for merchandise situated outside of the state. In brief, then, the possibility of adopting foreign charters, and of thus securing relief from part of the burden of Massachusetts taxation made the general corporation tax impracticable for a large number of corporations. Corporations whose property in Massachusetts consisted in intangible, more largely than in tangible, possessions as well as holding companies and corporations carrying on business in more than one state could reduce their taxes by obtaining a foreign charter. In order to retain these corporations to the state a revision of the tax laws was necessary.

To tax foreign and domestic corporations alike on their tangible property only and thus to equalize the tax was not a satisfactory solution, for the effect of such a change, as we have seen, would have been to impose a very much heavier tax on fifty per cent of Massachusetts corporations. The corporations that would be adversely affected thereby were already laboring under disadvantages and had for a long time complained of the burden of the tax on machinery.[1] Moreover, other states, like New York

---

[1] *Report of Tax Commission*, 1897, p. 56; *Report of Committee on Corporation Laws*, p. 57; 1898, *House Doc.* 1194, p. 4, petitions for the exemption of machinery in the cotton mills.

and Pennsylvania, were more lenient in the taxation of manufacturing and business corporations generally. For an industrial state like Massachusetts, it is more important to retain her industries than to add to its revenues by taxing them. On the other hand, to treat the second group of corporations like foreign corporations meant a loss to the state of over $450,000 in revenue.

The commissioners appointed to consider the laws relating to business corporations contented themselves with minor changes in taxation. They recommended (1) that in determining the corporate excess a deduction should be made for the value of merchandise taxed outside of the state; (2) that a deduction should be made also for the value of securities which were not taxable to a citizen of Massachusetts; and (3) that a minimum tax should be imposed on Massachusetts corporations equal to one-tenth of one per cent of the market value of their capital stock, from which, however, all other taxes paid by corporations in the state might be deducted.[1] The proposals of the commission were calculated to facilitate the activity of corporations engaging in business in several states, and to make possible holding companies for Massachusetts stocks.[2] Out of respect for the revenue involved, they refrained from any recommendation for the remedy of the chief evil which they had clearly shown, that is, the heavier burden on the more successful Massachusetts corporations. The legislature, however, met this situation with greater boldness. It set a limit to the taxes that might be imposed on corporations by making the maximum valuation on which a business corporation

[1] *Report of the Committee on Corporation Laws*, pp. 58 et seq.

[2] G. Calkins, "The Massachusetts Business Corporation Law," in Ripley, *Trusts, Pools and Corporations*, pp. 384-385.

might be taxed one hundred and twenty per cent of its tangible property.

II. *The Taxation of Business Corporations under the Law of 1903.*—It may be convenient at this point to sum up the law taxing business corporations, thus complicated by the legislation of 1903,[1] following the interpretation of the tax commissioner.[2] In the first place the real estate and machinery of such corporations are taxed locally.[3] The tax commissioner then determines the market value of the corporate franchise. This he does on the basis of stock quotations for the larger corporations. For the other companies his data are the report of the assets furnished by the companies and such other information as he may secure. To determine next the corporate excess, he makes the following deductions from the value of the capital stock: (1) real estate and (2) machinery, located in or out of the state; (3) other tangible property located out of the state, liable to taxation, whether taxed or not; (4) securities which are exempt to a citizen of Massachusetts. Whereas the deduction formerly made for property located outside of the state embraced only real estate and machinery, there is now exempted all tangible and intangible personalty situated outside of Massachusetts.[4] Furthermore, the law allows also the deduc-

---

[1] 1903, c. 437, §§ 71-74.

[2] *Report of Tax Commissioner* for 1905, pp. 19 *et seq.*

[3] The greater part of the taxes on business corporations is paid locally. In 1901 business corporations paid a total tax of $4,693,371. Of this amount nearly two-thirds, $3,006,794, was paid on real estate and machinery; and $1,686,577 on corporate excess. *Report of Committee on Corporation Laws*, p. 43. With the revision of the law in 1903 a still greater percentage of the total tax is paid directly to the local authorities.

[4] These additional deductions, as allowed by the tax commissioner in 1906, were $8,302,507 for securities and $18,083,264 for property situated

tion of securities exempt to Massachusetts citizens. By these are meant the stocks of Massachusetts corporations or other corporations which have been taxed in the state on their franchise, mortgages, and bonds exempt by statute. These deductions were intended to obviate all double taxation and to bring domestic corporations more to a level of equality with foreign corporations. For the purpose of making the deduction for real estate and machinery, the tax commissioner may be guided by the returns of the assessors. For property outside of the state his rule is: "If such property is liable to taxation, it should be deducted whether taxed or not."[1]

The amount remaining after these deductions have been made from the market value of the capital stock is the corporate excess. It is taxed, as before, at a rate determined by taking the per cent which the total tax, levied by the assessors in the state in any year on general property, forms of the total valuation of general property in the foregoing year. Since 1906, however, the average of the rates thus determined, for three years previous to the assessment, is taken.[2]

The taxes, however, that can be assessed on a corporation, both state and local, now have a maximum and a minimum limit. The minimum limit which a corporation must pay is one-tenth of one per cent of the market value of its capital stock. If so much is not due on property taxed by the local authorities, it is assessed by the tax commissioner. This minimum may be regarded as a payment for the bare right to exist and to carry on

outside of the state, together an amount equivalent to more than seven per cent of the corporate excess taxed. *Cf. Report of the Tax Commissioner* for 1906, p. 7.

[1] *Ibid.*, for 1905, p. 20.   [2] 1906, c. 271, § 12.

business as a corporation. To determine the maximum limit, a rather elaborate calculation is resorted to. A sum is taken equivalent to one hundred and twenty per cent of the tax commissioner's valuation of the real estate, machinery, tangible property, and securities taxable to citizens in Massachusetts. From this amount the value of all property taxed in the state or liable to taxation outside of the state is deducted. On the sum remaining, the tax commissioner assesses the corporation tax. The maximum amount on which the corporation is thus made liable to taxation, by both state and local authorities, is calculated on two elements: (1) the corporation's real estate, tangible property, and taxable securities, and (2) a valuation of its intangible property or franchise at a sum not to exceed one-fifth of the value of the items just enumerated.

The tax provisions of the law of 1903 have this significance. The majority of the Massachusetts corporations which had enjoyed an advantage in taxation over foreign corporations are left undisturbed. The additional deductions allowed would operate to make their position even more favorable. Corporations doing business in more than one state are no longer taxed for any property outside of Massachusetts. Holding companies, so far as they confine themselves to stocks in Massachusetts, pay only the tax of one-tenth of one per cent on the value of their capital. If, however, they should hold other stocks, or bonds, they would be taxed at a prohibitive rate.

The corporations which were formerly at a disadvantage for taxation on account of their Massachusetts charter, hold now a less unfavorable position relative to their foreign competitors. Excluding the minor items of taxable securities, they can not in any event be taxed for twenty per cent more than the foreign corporations.[1] The theory of the Massachusetts legislature evidently was that a slight additional burden would not suffice to induce Massachusetts corporations to incorporate in other states. The finality of such a solution would seem to be questionable. The recent joint committee on taxation speaks of domestic corporations still frequently finding it to their financial advantage to give up their Massachusetts charter, and to remedy this the committee proposes the obvious expedient of increasing the excise tax on foreign corporations.[2]

We have then for the taxation of business in Massachusetts three classes: (1) the individual and firm taxed locally, in theory of the law at least, on tangible and intangible property; (2) the foreign corporation taxable only on tangible property, and (3) the domestic corporation taxable, at the maximum, on an amount no greater than one hundred and twenty per cent of its tangible property, and, at the minimum, only for real estate and machinery.

The effect of the business corporation law of 1903 was certainly to encourage the formation of corporations in Massachusetts. This consequence cannot, however, well be ascribed to the tax provisions alone, since the entire system of corporation law has undergone revision. In the first year of the operation of the law, 1,000 corporations were organized with a capitalization of $66,623,-610 as against 259 with a capitalization of $11,590,460

[1] On the figures for 1901, disregarding taxable securities and merchandise located outside of the state, these corporations would by this compromise have saved the tax on $13,879,899 or $222,078. On the other hand, as foreign corporations they might have saved $451,758.

[2] *Report of Special Joint Committee on Taxation*, 1907, pp. 47-48.

for the previous year.[1] The number of additional foreign corporations filing organization papers has on the
other hand declined from the maximum in 1902, 631,
to 248 in 1906.[2]

From the point of view of revenue, the immediate
outcome was a considerable loss to the state and the
municipalities. The revenue from the general corporation tax was impaired in 1904, on account of the additional exemptions and the limitation of the tax on corporate excess, to the extent of $400,000. Thereafter,
however, the revenue from the general corporation tax
again increased so as to yield more than ever before.[3]
On the other hand the proportion of the tax paid by
business corporations, as compared with public-service
and financial corporations, has not increased, to a marked
degree, with the rapid growth of business corporations.[4]
Business corporations pay only about thirty per cent of
the amount assessed under the general corporation tax.

[1] See annual *Reports of Tax Commissioner*, particularly for 1906, pp.
13–17.

[2] *Report of the Committee on Corporation Laws*, p. 19, and the annual
Reports of the Tax Commissioner.

[3] The additional deduction under the new law for exempt securities
and property liable to taxation out of the state, amounted to $15,219,499,
and the loss on the tax occasioned thereby in 1904 was $252,644. How
much was lost to the state by the operation of the maximum limit, the
tax commissioner does not say, but it amounted to something less than
$208,825.85. On the other hand, new revenues were created by the
organization of corporations, and by the new excise on foreign corporations, yielding in all about $65,000. *Ibid.*, for 1904, pp. 21–24.

[4] *Cf.* table *supra*, p. 61, and the *Tax Commissioners' Reports*, from
which the following figures for the taxes assessed on corporate excess
are taken:

	Total.	Business Corporations.	Per cent.
1904	$5,166,900	1,567,943	30.
1905	5,856,487	1,791,686	30.
1906	6,103,557	1,973,701	32.

The tendency for business to adopt corporate form threatens to make some inroads into the revenues of municipalities from the general property tax, especially when the firms incorporating are trading companies. This has proved to be the case in Boston. Statistics prepared by the assessors show that beginning with 1884, firms with an assessed valuation at the time of their incorporation of $20,307,300 have become corporations. In 1906 they were assessed locally on but $1,778,400 or one-twelfth. As a result of this movement to incorporate, a sum equal to nearly two per cent of the total valuation is excluded from local taxation. [1]

As in the case of trading corporations little beyond the real estate is taxable, the result is a heavy loss to municipalities, unless the owners of the corporation reside where the business is carried on. From some of its largest corporations Boston receives no tax at all. Considering only firms originally assessed at $200,000 or more, which had become corporations in the period from 1887 to and including 1905, the aggregate of the original assessments for Boston was $7,480,900. In 1905 these were locally assessed on $342,800. Of the total tax paid by them to the state for the same year ($108,189) Boston received two-fifths ($48,605) and Brookline one-fourth ($25,796). Even including Boston's tax on the locally assessed property, the city lost more than one-

[1] The movement in the direction of incorporation did not however assume considerable proportions till 1895:

	Assessed at time of incorporation.	Assessed in 1906.
1895–1900	$6,432,400	$703,500
1901–1905	8,451,900	502,200
1895–1905	$14,884,300	$1,205,700

half of the tax on these corporations. Speaking of this experience of Boston, the mayor says : [1]

It is nothing short of a monstrous wrong to the citizens of Boston, that our corporation law allows people to compel Boston's taxpayers to furnish police and fire protection for millions of property, and pay all other expenses falling upon the city through the property being located here, while the taxes on nearly all that property (and in some cases on all of it) are either paid to other cities and towns, or else not paid at all.

He advocated therefore before the legislature that such corporations be taxed on their tangible personalty, as foreign corporations are taxed, and that the property taxed locally be deducted from the value of the capital stock in determining the corporate excess.

As we have seen, the motive for reducing the tax on the corporate excess of Massachusetts corporations was not the realization that the corporations affected could not afford the tax, but rather that these corporations could avoid paying by assuming a foreign charter. Accordingly, it would seem proper to alter the tax so as to relieve only such corporations as would suffer by the competition of corporations under foreign charter. For this purpose a distinction should be made between manufacturing and trading corporations. Exemption or relief to the manufacturing corporations, which are otherwise at a disadvantage, would be in keeping with the industrial interests of the state, and in line with the policy of other states which favor manufacturing corporations.

In the case of trading companies, however, the market is local, and there is therefore less ground for fearing

[1] *Boston Post*, Aug. 15, 1906; *Cf.* 1906, *House Doc.* 348.

that taxation will drive them out of the state. Moreover, they can not find relief in adopting a foreign charter, for as foreign companies these corporations would pay a tax on their stock in trade. There seems to be no reason why such corporations should be favored over both foreign corporations and individuals or firms. To tax them at least on their stock in trade would seem to be as proper as to tax manufacturing companies on their machinery.

The special committee on taxation of 1907, realizing this situation and heeding the protest against the present distribution of the tax, proposed two changes in the mode of taxing business corporations. It recommended that for mercantile corporations, the minimum tax should be levied on an amount equal to the value of the merchandise, and further that the revenue from these corporations be returned to the municipalities in which these corporations are located. Taxation of these corporations, according to their sworn returns to the tax commissioner, the committee regarded as a better method of arriving at the proper valuation than the local assessor's estimate.[1]

Cause for further criticism is to be found in the manner in which the tax operates first on property, and second on income. We have seen that for a large number of corporations, the value of their real estate and machinery exceeds the market value of their capital stock. These pay the local tax on real estate and machinery, while their other property, tangible and intangible, escapes. Corporations whose corporate excess is less than the value of their merchandise likewise do not pay on all their tangible property. For both of these groups sixty per cent of their merchandise escaped taxation in 1901.

[1] *Report*, pp. 42-46.

There remains then only the group of corporations whose property is largely in intangible form, and these corporations pay on all their tangible property, and also on a part of their intangible property. From the point of view of the taxation of property, Massachusetts business corporations largely escape a tax on the full value of their tangible property, and only a small amount of intangible property is reached. The corporation tax thus proves itself but an inapt instrument for the taxation of property, even tangible property, and, by so much the more, for the taxation of intangible property.

The failure of the tax to reach property regardless of its income-earning capacity would not be a serious criticism, if it could be shown that the tax is proportional to earnings arising from the property. Assuming for the moment that the value of the shares represents the capitalized net income, it would appear that corporations, in which the value of the shares is less than that of their property taxed locally, pay in taxes more than is justified by the net earnings of their investments. On the other hand, in the case of those corporations for which the tax would be largely in excess of the tax on property, namely the most successful corporations, the law restricts the tax on the corporate excess. The basis of the tax thus becomes less than the capitalization of net income. The tax would then seem to act regressively, its greatest burden being imposed on the weakest, and its least burden on the strongest corporations.[1] In fact, however, net assets,

---

[1] For a full discussion of the inequalities inherent in the present method of taxing business corporations, see *Report of Tax Commissioner* for 1905, pp. 22–27. Thus of two corporations with a capital stock having the same value, one having its capital invested in tangible property might pay twenty times as much as another whose assets were of an intangible character. See p. 27.

and not a market valuation, form the real measure of the tax for a great many corporations. Here the objections are the same as to the property tax, namely that the tax measured by tangible property is not necessarily the same as a tax on the income arising from the property.

Another criticism of the tax on business corporations is one applicable to the general corporation tax as it applies to all corporations, namely, that the value of the corporation for taxation is determined on the inadequate basis of capital stock alone. This must necessarily introduce inequality as between corporations, and invite evasion of a part or even of the whole of the tax through the creation of indebtedness. One Boston corporation which had been locally assessed in Boston as a firm in 1896 for $837,000 paid in 1904 and 1905 no tax as a corporation either to the state or to Boston. Another cause of inequality is the greater opportunity afforded to corporations whose capital is invested in merchandise to offset tangible property by debts, as compared with corporations whose chief assets are locally taxable machinery.[1] To prevent evasion through the creation of indebtedness, the special joint committee of 1907 proposed to require the corporation in its sworn returns to the tax commissioner to state the amount of its debts, and furthermore to state that no debts were created for the purpose of reducing taxes.[2]

From an administrative point of view, the complicated basis for calculating the tax on corporate excess and the additional deductions allowed would seem to make the tax in no small degree dependent on self-assessment.

[1] *Cf.* F. A. North, *Business Corporations in Massachusetts*, 1903. One section in this book is headed: "Incorporation as a legal method of reducing taxes."

[2] *Report*, pp. 51, 52.

For a great many corporations there are no market quotations, and the value of their stocks must be determined from their returns.   While for real estate and machinery the tax commissioner has the valuation of the local assessor, for merchandise and taxable securities he has not even the assessor's estimate to guide him.[1]

To sum up, it may be said that business corporations are very largely taxed on their tangible property only, and that with the privilege allowed to corporations of deducting their debts, they are for the most part taxed for less than their tangible assets.   Only to a small extent is the value of the corporation in excess of its tangible property reached.   In the case of business corporations the endeavors to reach intangible property seem to have had little more success than the similar attempts to tax intangible personal estate to individuals.

It would seem fair to conclude that the taxation of business corporations is proportional neither to property nor to income.   It is not an adequate means of reaching either tangible or intangible property; it is not levied with respect to tax-paying ability as measured by capitalized earnings.   Nevertheless, in the face of the practical situation, it is superior to the mere property tax, laxly administered.

III. *Taxation of Corporations to engage in Business in other States.*—Corporations organized to do business in other states were not given special attention for purposes of taxation with the exception of mining and oil companies, and later companies to build railroads and telegraphs in foreign countries.   The mining boom, through which the country was passing at the time the

---

[1] For a criticism of the tax provisions of the law of 1903, see also a pamphlet by H. Winn, *The Corporation Exemptions of 1903.*

general corporation tax was enacted, suggested the taxation of mining companies, and a semi-annual tax of
seven-twelfths of one per cent was imposed in 1864 on
their stock.   From this tax all other taxes paid in Massachusetts or elsewhere might be deducted.[1]   This law
sought in effect to tax these corporations like other corporations.   In the next year foreign mining corporations
located in the state, as well as domestic corporations,
were taxed, this time by levying a semi-annual tax of
one-twentieth of one per cent of the par value of their
stock, and also an annual tax of four per cent on their
profits.   The tax on profits was abolished for foreign
companies.[2]   The effect of the tax was to destroy a great
number of purely speculative companies.   The yield
dwindled from $34,191 in 1864 to $9,045 in 1870, and to
about one-half of this sum in the next decade.   With the
mining boom at the beginning of the eighties the tax
rose again to $15,575 in 1880, and $30,612 in 1883.   In
the latter year the rate of the tax on foreign corporations was reduced to one-fortieth of one per cent semi-
annually, and a maximum of $300 was set to the tax,
and in the next year the basis of the tax was changed
from the par value of the stocks to the amount paid in.
The income again dwindled to $5,267 in 1884, to increase
to $15,306 in 1899, and $21,011 in 1900, with the mining
boom of that date.[3]

Corporations to construct railroads and telegraphs in
foreign countries were subjected to the same tax as mining companies, that is, one-twentieth of one per cent
semi-annually on the par value of their capital and four

[1] 1864, c. 208, §§ 10, 11.

[2] 1865, c. 283, §§ 8–10 : 1866, c. 291, § 2 ; 1867, c. 299.

[3] 1882, c. 106, § 4 ; 1883, c. 74.

per cent of the dividends.[1] In 1895 the rate was reduced to one-twentieth of one per cent per annum.[2] This tax was found to be prohibitive for such corporations and, as a result, only one corporation of this character was formed under Massachusetts charter.[3]

By the act of 1903 these corporations are treated either as domestic or foreign corporations according to their charter. As foreign corporations they are subject to the tax of one-hundredth of one per cent of the par value of their authorized capital stock and the maximum of the tax is $2,000. As domestic corporations they are allowed deductions for all their property liable to taxation out of the state. Possessing little tangible property in the state, their tax would probably be one-tenth of one per cent of the market value of their capital stock, as determined by the tax commissioner,—the minimum tax levied by the state on its corporations. Even this minimum tax would not serve to attract large corporations to seek a Massachusetts charter, as the annual tax would still be very heavy as compared with that imposed by New Jersey.[4]

Corporations owning ships and vessels engaged in the foreign carrying trade are taxed at the rate of one-third of one per cent of the value of such property. The value of such ships and vessels is then deducted in de-

[1] 1879, c. 274, § 6.   [2] 1895, c. 300.

[3] For the weight of the general corporation tax on corporations doing business outside of the state, see *Report of the Committee on Corporation Laws*, p. 54 *et seq*. For the effect of the Massachusetts tax laws in deterring corporations from organizing in the state, see testimony of C. F. Adams in *Hearings relating to Taxation*, 1894, p. 132; see also p. 160.

[4] The Committee on Corporation Laws estimated that even this minimum would impose on the United States Steel Corporation a tax in Massachusetts ten times the amount paid under the New Jersey law. *Report*, p. 63.

termining the corporate excess. The same treatment is accorded to this class of property owned by individuals and firms. Ships in the foreign carrying trade have long been treated more leniently than other property for purposes of taxation.[1]

IV. *Foreign Corporations.*—Foreign corporations were taxed not under any specific provision of the law, but only under the general law of taxation. Under the general law real estate, machinery, and stock in trade, are made taxable without regard to the residence of the owner, and the effect of this provision and of court decisions is to make corporations taxable only for their tangible property in the state.[2] The recent committee on taxation proposes to amend the law so as to tax explicitly foreign corporations on their personal property situated within the commonwealth.[3]

Not until 1903[4] were foreign corporations in general, subjected to an excise tax, and then the tax was imposed for the purpose of obtaining proper returns from such corporations rather than for revenue.[5] The rate of the tax was made one-hundredth of one per cent of the par value of the authorized capital stock. From this tax the taxes paid locally in Massachusetts are deducted and the maximum amount of the excise is fixed at $2,000.[6] The

[1] 1902, c. 374, § 2.

[2] *R. L.*, c. 12, § 23; 1903, c. 437, § 71; 158 Mass. 461; 161 Mass. 326. The latter case defines "stock in trade" as the "visible and tangible property with which the trade or business of the owner is carried on and to which it relates." *Report of the Committee on Corporation Laws*, pp. 35-37.

[3] *Report*, p. 48 *et seq.*   [4] Unless under 1864, c. 208, § 2.

[5] 1903, 437, § 75. *Report of the Committee on Corporation Laws*, p. 62; G. Calkins, "The Massachusetts Business Corporation Law," in Ripley, *Trusts, Pools and Corporations*, pp. 385, 386.

[6] 188 Mass. 1.

relative advantages for taxation enjoyed by foreign and domestic corporations have already been noted, and it will be remembered that for the most part the advantage accrues to the domestic corporation. To impose a high excise on foreign corporations, in order to deprive these of the advantage which, under certain circumstances mentioned before, they enjoy over domestic corporations, would, it was feared, deter foreign corporations from coming into the state and result in greater economic loss than financial gain.[1] The special committee on taxation of 1907, however, in its report, recommends that the excise be increased to one-fiftieth of one per cent, and that the maximum of the excise be raised to $5,000.[2] More proper would seem to be the taxation of foreign corporations on so much of their capital stock as is invested in Massachusetts in the same way as domestic corporations. There would then be one general law for the taxation of business corporations.

The proposal has been repeatedly made to compel foreign corporations located in Massachusetts to make returns of their stockholders in the state and thus to assist the local assessor in taxing their shares.[3] This measure has been opposed on the ground that it would drive many such corporations, especially mining corporations, from the state, and deprive the community of the large benefits incident to their activity in Massachusetts. It is urged that the mere agitation for such a law has had the effect of preventing corporations intending to engage in business outside of the state from organizing in the state.[4]

[1] See J. M. Hallowell, op. cit., p. 18.   [2] Report, p. 47.

[3] See e. g., 1890, House Doc. 326; 1900, House Doc. 854; Hearings before the Joint Special Committee on Taxation, 1894, p. 132.

[4] See 1900, House Doc. 1378, and Report of the Committee on Taxation, 1898 (House Doc. 1259), p. 41.

The revenue from the excise on the foreign corporations yielded $48,820 in 1904, and $46,292 in 1906. With more adequate facilities for enforcing this tax, it is believed that this sum can be at least doubled.[1]

V. *Incorporation Fees.*—The charges imposed for the privilege of incorporation have undergone an interesting development in Massachusetts. Originally the incorporation fee was merely a charge for recording the certificate of incorporation, and the fee, one dollar, was the same as the fee for recording other corporation papers.[2] Two years later the amount was increased to five dollars.[3] In 1870, however, the payment was graduated according to a presumed amount of benefit, measured by the authorized capital stock. The rate was made one-twentieth of one per cent of the capital stock.[4] The next year the maximum charge was made $200 and the minimum five dollars.[5]

In the business corporation law of 1903 which sought to facilitate the formation of corporations, the incorporation fee was reduced, the rate being made one-fortieth of one per cent. The minimum charge was, however, raised to ten dollars.[6] The tax commissioner in his report for 1906, and likewise the recent special committee on taxation, advocated the restoration of the former rate of the charge for incorporation, and that at the same

[1] *Report of the Joint Special Committee on Taxation*, 1907, p. 23.

[2] 1863, c. 231, § 2.   [3] 1865, c. 76, § 1.

[4] 1870, c. 224, § 59.   [5] 1871, c. 356.

[6] 1903, c. 437, § 88. Foreign corporations are required to pay, before transacting business, a fee of twenty-five dollars for filing a copy of their charter, by-laws, and other papers. Foreign and domestic corporations are further charged a fee of five dollars for filing other papers. *Ibid.*, § 91. The revenue from the incorporation fees and other corporation fees amounted in 1905 to $66,373 on domestic corporations, and $8,810 on foreign corporations.

time the minimum fee be increased. This change is favored as a means both of increasing the revenue and of checking the formation of undesirable corporations.[1]

[1] *Report of the Joint Special Committee on Taxation*, 1907, pp. 50–51; *Report of Tax Commissioner* for 1906, pp. 15, 16.

CHAPTER V

Taxation of Public-Service Corporations

In the taxation of public-service corporations, there are evidences in the Massachusetts law of three stages, exemption from taxation for the purpose of encouragement, taxation as ordinary corporate enterprises, and finally, special taxation for a special franchise. The early practice of exempting the property of corporations to which the right of eminent domain had been granted, such as turnpikes, canals, aqueducts, evidently had for its aim the encouragement of public works. It is true that the shares of such corporations were early made taxable, but it appears that originally the property of other corporations was taxed to the corporations, and in addition, the shares were taxed again to their owners.[1] Public-service corporations were thus taxed more leniently.

Taxation was in fact more favorable to public-service than to other corporations also under the general corporation tax. In the case of the other corporations, which until recently were chiefly manufacturing companies, the local taxation of real estate and machinery reached most of their assets. After the general corporation tax was adopted, provision had been made for the fuller taxation of other elements that entered into the market value of their shares. In the case of railroads, however, the exemption of much real estate reduced the basis for local taxation, and the bonded debt made the

---

[1] *Vide supra*, p. 14.

value of the capital stock alone an inadequate measure
of the value of the corporate property. Likewise in the
case of street railways the real estate alone was taxed
locally; the other equipment could be reached only
through the shares, and was exempt to the extent that
it was represented by bonds. The result was, and the
same seems still to be true, that public-service corporations were taxed on less than the value of their tangible
property.

More recently a conscious distinction for purposes of
taxation has been made between public and private industrial corporations. In 1903 the general corporation
tax was revised with a view to taxing business corporations on little more than their tangible property
at the utmost. On the other hand, public-service corporations were left under the general corporation tax.
The underlying motive was to tax such corporations
for all elements of profit that register themselves in the
market value of the shares. Another consideration here
is the fact that so much of the tangible property of
these companies is exempt from local assessment. The
general corporation tax, in its original form has thus
become a tax on public-service corporations and financial institutions.

Earlier, however, a movement for the special taxation
of public-service corporations, on their franchise had set
in. It is to be borne in mind that, on the one hand, no
compensation is required in Massachusetts when the
franchise is granted, but that, on the other hand, the
companies are not permitted to capitalize the value of
the franchise they possess.[1] Beginning with the nine-

---

[1] *Cf.* W. Z. Ripley, "The Capitalization of Public Service Corporations," in his *Trusts, Pools and Corporations*, c. vii, and particularly
p. 139.

ties,[1] when electricity had brought into prominence street railway, telephone, and electric light companies, a demand arose for a payment, whether in lump sum or through annual taxation, for the special opportunities of profit which these corporations were believed to enjoy.[2]   As these companies were using the public ways,[3] this agitation often took the form of a demand of a payment for the use of the streets,[4] but more recently the special opportunity for profit has been emphasized. The demand was loudest in the instance of the most prominent of this class of corporations, the street railways.   As early as 1892 the Boston Rapid Transit Commission proposed that these companies be required to divide with the public their earnings in excess of a stipulated dividend, and in 1898 a proposal of this kind was enacted into law.[5]   Since that date there has been an agitation for the special taxation of other public-service corporations, gas and electric companies, telephone and telegraph companies.[6]   In the case of Massachusetts, with its careful control over the capitalization of public-service corporations, such a method of collecting a return for special opportunities of profit, by which the interest of the

[1] See for example 1891, *House Doc.* 487, 505, 524, 545; 1893, *House Doc.* 636, 638; 1895, *Sen. Doc.* 14; 1897, *House Doc.* 445.

[2] See address of Governor Russel, 1890, *Sen. Doc.* 1, pp. 26, 27.

[3] W. S. Allen, *Development of Street Railways in the Commonwealth of Massachusetts* (pamphlet), p. 25.

[4] 1902, c. 342, sought to satisfy this demand by making underground conduits, wires and pipes laid in the streets by corporations other than street railways taxable where located.

[5] *Report of the Rapid Transit Commission*, Boston, 1892, pp. 116-119.

[6] 1900, *House Doc.* 1240, and a similar bill every year thereafter, for a graduated tax on gross receipts; 1902, *House Doc.* 900, 1326; 1903, *House Doc.* 942, 1417, 1491; 1904, *House Doc.* 828; 1905, *House Doc.* 514; 1906, *House Doc.* 891.

public is made coördinate with that of the corporation, may perhaps prove effective.[1] Thus far, however, the special tax on street railways has remained a mere threat.

I. *The General Corporation Tax and Public-Service Corporations.*—Public-service corporations are therefore still taxed under the general corporation tax, in its original form. The general corporation tax in effect makes the market valuation of the stocks the taxable valuation of the corporations. In Massachusetts the market quotations of securities would be less objectionable as a measure of the taxable value of public-service corporations than elsewhere. It has been the policy of the state to supervise carefully the issue of securities, and these have been limited to actual investment.[2] The value of securities is, therefore, apt to be less influenced by speculative manipulation, and thus tends to measure more accurately the value of the corporation.[3] For taxation, however, not the value of all the securities outstanding is made the basis of the tax, but only the value of the capital stock. The fact that the railroads and street railways were originally built through the issue of stock rather than bonds made the capital stock a less objectionable basis for the tax. Moreover the older conception that bonds are a debt, rather than a preferred interest in the corporation, suggested exemption originally, and still stands as an obstacle in the path of reform.[4] More important a factor, however, is the increase of the tax which would result thereby.

---

[1] See W. Z. Ripley, *op. cit.*, c. vii; see, however, pp. 145, 146.

[2] *Ibid.*, pp. 121, 129.

[3] *Ibid.*, p. 129; *Cf. Report of the Ontario Commission on the Taxation of Railways*, 1905, p. 117 ; *Report of the California Commission on Revenue and Taxation*, 1906, p. 115, also 111–114.

[4] See the remarks of the Tax Commissioner, Mr. Trefry, in the *Report of the Ontario Commission*, p. 122.

The taxation of public-service corporations on the value of stocks alone is defective therefore in several respects. In the first place criticism is to be directed against the basis of taxation. Public-service corporations, particularly railroads and street railways, are heavily bonded. Since the tax is based on the value of stocks only, the productive property represented by bonds is exempted. Incident to this disregard of indebtedness in taxation is necessarily an inequality both as between groups of public-service corporations, and also as between different corporations of the same group; for the relation of bonded debt to capital stock varies. Thus street railways are heavily bonded but electric companies are not, and gas companies are bonded to a still smaller extent. From the point of view of either property or income, the present basis of taxation is therefore not only inadequate but also inequitable.

Reform here must, however, entail hardship. The adoption of the broader and more proper basis for taxation, the valuation of both stock and bonds, would necessarily increase taxation, and the weight of the increase would fall on the shareholders and not on the bondholders. In order to obviate a sudden change the recent special committee on taxation proposes to include in the taxable valuation of public-service corporations only future issues of bonds,[1] whether newly emitted or merely refunded, and also so much of the unfunded debt as is incurred for property.[2] While this plan has

[1] *Report*, pp. 31–35. The committee thought that an immediate change would increase the taxes of the railroads by fifty per cent, and that in the case of some gas and street railway companies it would cause virtual bankruptcy. See p. 34.

[2] The creation of floating indebtedness for the purpose of construction and equipment has been resorted to by public-service corporations to evade the restrictions imposed on the issue of securities. See *Bureau of Census, Special Reports, Street and Electric Railways*, 1902, p. 93.

the merit of not disturbing the shareholders suddenly, it would tend to prolong the existing inequalities for a considerable period.[1]

Even if both stocks and bonds are made the basis of taxation, the general corporation tax is not an ideal method of taxing public-service corporations. It has indeed the merit of reaching elements other than mere property which give value to a public-service corporation. Moreover, the machinery provided—the market valuation—is simpler than assessment by a special board. Furthermore, the market valuation under the conditions imposed by Massachusetts may be regarded as roughly the capitalization of net earnings. Its defect, however, is that it levies as great, and no greater, a percentage on the capitalization which represents only normal profits as on the capitalization which stands for extraordinary profits, where the franchise confers opportunities for special gains. Manifestly it is just for the community to exact a greater percentage of the earnings due to a special monopoly privilege granted to a corporation, than of profits which are not due to any extraordinary opportunity created by the community. It would thus be necessary to supplement the method of taxing corporations on their capital stock and bonds with a special tax which would reach monopoly profits, where such exist, either by a division of earnings after a certain dividend has been reached, or by some other device.

---

[1] Professor Bullock proposes that pending radical change the corporate excess be determined by deducting from the market value of the capital stock not all of the property taxed locally, but only so much as corresponds to the proportion which the market value of the capital stock bears to the market value of the bonds. "Taxation of Corporations in Massachusetts," *Quarterly Journal of Economics*, vol. xxi, p. 238. The effect would be to increase slightly the taxes of corporations with little bonded debt, but to increase rather considerably the tax of heavily bonded corporations.

In point of fact, public-service corporations are with few exceptions still taxed for less than their tangible property. The older policy of refraining from utilizing corporations as a source of gain to the community still obtains in fact if not in theory. The drift of sentiment is, however, in the opposite direction. The policy of lenient taxation would of course be justified if the reduced tax were compensated for by cheaper service.[1] The danger here is, however, as Governor Wolcott,[2] and more recently Governor Bates,[3] pointed out, that the special advantage in taxation may be capitalized to the profit of the shareholder rather than be transferred to the community in reduced prices for service. This is particularly apt to be the case where the charge for service is at a customary rate, as in the case of street railways, or where the advantage in taxation is not sufficient to justify any appreciable difference in the price of the service.

II. *Fiscal Importance of the Tax on Public Service Corporations.*—From the point of view of revenue, as we have already pointed out in considering the general corporation tax,[4] the largest share of the yield from the general corporation tax comes from public-service corporations. This is due chiefly to the fact, noticed before, that most corporate property is not taxed locally and is therefore represented in the corporate excess. Thus, for 1906, railroads were assessed $93,120,000 on real estate taxed locally, and $95,000,000 on their corporate excess.[5] For

---

[1] For this view, see *Report of the Railroad Commissioners* for 1895, pp. III, 112.

[2] 1897, *Sen. Doc.* I, pp. 28-30; *cf.* also 1891, *Sen. Doc.* I, pp. 26, 27.

[3] *Mass. Acts and Resolves* for 1903, pp. 607, 608.

[4] *Vide supra*, p. 61.

[5] See Bullock, *op. cit.*, p. 219; *Report of the Joint Special Committee on Taxation*, 1907, p. 36.

1905 street railways paid $979,000 on their corporate excess and only about $535,000 on their locally assessed property. Electric companies paid for the year 1904 a total tax of $598,000 and gas companies paid $507,000. Of these sums gas companies paid on corporate excess only $59,379, and part of $23,438 paid by gas and electric companies, whereas electric companies paid $193,091.[1] The fact that corporate excess represents to a very great extent property exempted from local taxation has of course given special justification for complaint against the present method of distributing the tax on the corporate excess of public-service companies.[2]

There are two periods in the activity of public-service corporations, and this reflects itself both in the amount of revenue and in the corporations which contributed the revenue, as is shown by the table on the following page. In the first period, up to about 1890, over three-fourths of the revenue from public-service corporations came from the railroads. The second period dates from the use of electricity in urban and inter-urban transportation and in electric lighting, and the extension of the telephone. Between 1885 and 1890 the tax on the corporate excess of electric companies increased tenfold; that on the corporate excess of telephone and street railway companies more than doubled. In the decade elaps-

---

[1] Telegraph and telephone companies were assessed locally in 1906 for property valued at $10,176,931 (*ibid.*), which would make the local tax about $170,000. These companies paid on their corporate excess in 1906 $466,000, so that nearly three-fourths of their taxes is collected by the state.

[2] While for public-service corporations more than one-half of the tax is levied on corporate excess, only about one-third of the tax levied on other corporations is paid on corporate excess. For 1891 the figures were respectively $1,686,000 and $3,006,000. *Cf. Report of the Committee on Corporation Laws*, p. 43.

ing between 1893 and 1903 the tax collected by the state from electric companies became more than four times as great; that from street railways nearly tripled, and that from telephone and telegraph companies doubled in amount.

REVENUE FROM PUBLIC-SERVICE CORPORATIONS

(In thousands of dollars.)

	1871.	1875.	1880.	1885.	1890.	1893.	1903.	1905.
Total public service	827	689	826	1,082	1,905	2,250	3,414	3,585
Light, heat, power etc., (total)	25	36	43	56	106	94	261	330
Gas	19	34	40	40	62	43	62	44
Gas and electric	..	..	..	..	..	..	17	26
Electric	..	..	..	2	23	38	159	250
Water	4	1	3	13	20	12	10	8
Transportation and transmission (total)	802	652	782	1,023	1,798	2,156	2,932	3,254
Railroad	747	586	659	840	1,365	1,496	1,594	1,708
Street railway	47	38	68	90	212	333	976	979
Steam boat	2	20	20	34	61	68	91	80
Telegraph	5	7	13	0.6	0.6	20	..	..
Telephone	..	..	20	58	159	238	..	..
Telegraph and telephone	..	..	..	..	..	..	481	486
Per cent of total paid by railroads	90	85	80	77	71	66	46	47

The tax on railroads still remains, nevertheless, the chief source of income, yielding in 1905 over forty-seven per cent of the total revenue assessed by the tax commissioner on public-service corporations. The street railways contributed in 1905 more than twenty-seven per cent; telegraph and telephone companies over thirteen per cent, and electric companies more than seven per cent; steamboat, gas, and water companies, paid the rest. From the point of view of revenue, public-service corporations contributed in 1905 sixty per cent of the taxes assessed by the tax commissioner under the general corporation tax. The amount paid by public-service corporations above their local taxes was, in 1905, about one-third of the taxes other than those on real estate and machinery assessed on all corporations. The public-service corporations thus contribute a very considerable proportion of the total taxes on corporations.

The significance of taxation for public-service corporations, and the problems involved, can be seen more clearly in the detailed discussion. For street railways the data available are more satisfactory than for other public-service companies, and the problems involved can be studied to better advantage. We shall therefore turn our attention first to the taxation of street railways.

III. *Street Railways.*—Street railways did not assume very great importance in Massachusetts until electricity was introduced as a motive power. Beginning with 1887, "when electricity was demonstrated to be a practical form of traction and a probable commercial success," in a period of ten years about fifteen hundred miles of street railway were equipped, while horse cars dwindled from more than five hundred miles to less than thirty.[1] Since that date the development has continued, until in 1905 nearly twenty-seven hundred miles of street railway were in operation.[2]

As street railways are not regarded as manufacturing companies, their equipment, rails, cars, wires, etc., are not assessed locally, but are taxed only as they enter into the value of the shares.[3] The result is that only a

[1] *Report of the Special Committee appointed to investigate the Relations between Cities and Towns and Street Railway Companies,* 1898, p. 65.

[2] *Thirty-seventh Annual Report of the Board of Railroad Commissioners* (1906), p. 37.

[3] 8 Allen 330. *Report of the Joint Special Committee on Taxation,* 1894, p. 28.

small part of their property is taxed in the cities and towns where the street railways operate. Thus the local taxes amounted to about $475,000 in 1904 and $535,000 in 1905, whereas the tax on corporate excess amounted to $906,000 in 1904 and to $979,000 in 1905.

Beginning in 1890, soon after electricity had brought about a remarkable extension of street railways, a demand arose for a change in the system of taxation. The complaint was of a twofold character. In the first place, the method of distributing the tax on the corporate excess of street railways often apportioned the proceeds to towns and cities other than those from which the companies derived their earnings. In the second place, a demand was made that a special payment be exacted either through taxation or in a lump sum for the special privilege conferred on these corporations.[1] The question was submitted for consideration to the Boston Rapid Transit Commission, then dealing with Boston's street railway problem.

The commission proposed, as a remedy, to tax locally not only real estate and machinery, but also the cars and the equipment in the street. In this way it sought to overcome the injustice involved in the mode of distribution of the tax then employed. Tentatively it proposed also, that after dividends reached eight per cent, street railways should be required to pay to the municipalities a sum equal to the dividends in excess of eight per cent.[2] The first recommendation would have increased the tax on railways considerably. Neither of the changes pro-

---

[1] See 1890, *House Doc.* 513, 576; Gov. Robinson's Messages, 1891, *Sen. Doc.* 1, pp. 26, 27; 1892, *Sen. Doc.* 1, p. 42, and 1891, *House Docs.* 487, 505, 524, 545.

[2] *Report of the Boston Rapid Transit Commission*, 1892, pp. 116–119, 281; 1893, *House Doc.* 976.

posed was adopted. A later special committee of the legislature advocated the distribution of the tax on corporate excess according to the location of the railways, but even this change was not made.[1] In 1894, however, when the Boston Elevated Railway Company was incorporated, provision was made for the payment of a franchise tax beginning in 1907 of from one to five per cent of the gross earnings in addition to its taxes as a street railway.[2]

The agitation for a special franchise tax, or some other method of compensation to the cities and towns from the street railways, continued,[3] and this problem, together with the whole question of the relation of cities and towns to street railways was submitted to a special committee appointed by the governor. This committee pointed out that the demand for a special franchise tax rested on the belief that street railways enjoyed " public franchises of 'unusual value," and were making " inordinately large profits." In its opinion, however, the street railway business yielded " with skillful and prudent management only a fair average return."[4] The committee expressed its general satisfaction with the corporation tax as it operated in the case of the street railways, recommending however that the method of distributing the tax be changed, so as to give the proceeds to the cities and towns in which the railways operated.

---

[1] *Report of the Special Joint Committee on Taxation*, 1894, pp. 27–29.

[2] 1894, c. 548, §§ 16, 21 ; 1897, c. 500, § 10.

[3] See Gov. Wolcott's address ; 1897, *Sen. Doc.* 1, pp. 28–30. *Report of the Railroad Commissioners* for 1895, pp. 111 and 112.

[4] *Report of the Special Committee on Cities and Towns and Street Railway Companies*, p. 36, citing *Report of the Railroad Commissioners* for 1896, p. 110.

Following in the footsteps of the earlier commission, the committee proposed that a special franchise tax be imposed on companies which had paid an average of six per cent in dividends since their organization. Whenever such companies declare a dividend in excess of eight per cent, they are to pay, as a special franchise tax, for the benefit of the municipalities, a sum equal to the dividends in excess of eight per cent. In this way the committee sought to make the community a partner in the extraordinary profits of the corporation. Such a plan, the committee argued, would not be open to the same criticism as the limitation of dividends; it would not hamper enterprise or prevent improvement, but on the contrary this policy would encourage better service for the sake of increased profits.

Being a public-service corporation, owned and operated for private profit, it seems just and in accordance with sound principles that, when the private ownership has received a reasonable return upon its investment, the public should share, through a form of special taxation, in the increment of profit, provided it can do so without danger of offering an inducement to those in control of the property to stint or conceal their profits.[1]

The committee further recommended a graduated tax on the gross receipts to defray the cost of removing ice and snow, and of widening and keeping in repair the streets—a payment for special service rather than a tax. This was no new burden but, in the main, a commutation of work to a money payment. These recommendations were enacted into law in 1898.[2]

[1] *Report of the Special Committee on Cities and Towns and Street Railway Companies*, pp. 38, 39.

[2] 1898, c. 578.

Street railways[1] are thus taxable locally on their real estate and machinery. They are further taxable on the value of their capital stock in excess of the property which is locally assessed, at the rate levied on corporate excess.[2] Whenever a street railway, which has paid an average of six per cent since its organization, declares a dividend in excess of eight per cent, it is required to pay as an additional franchise tax a sum equal to the dividend in excess of eight per cent.[3] These taxes are assessed by the tax commissioner, and are then distributed among the municipalities. The basis is the percentage of the total length of the track of a company located in the cities and towns in which it operates.[4] In addition, street railways pay the so-called commutation tax. This tax is assessed and collected locally, the rate varying from one per cent of the gross receipts for companies whose annual receipts are $4,000 per mile or less to three per cent for companies whose gross receipts are $28,000 per mile. The proceeds of this tax must be applied to the maintenance of the public roads where the tracks are located.[5]

The Boston Elevated is taxed in a slightly different way. It pays, in lieu of this commutation tax and special franchise tax, a tax of seven-eighths of one per cent of the

---

[1] The law regulating the taxation of street railways is now summed up in 1906, c. 463, pt. iii, §§ 125-137.

[2] Interstate street railways are taxed on such a proportion of the capital stock as their line in the state forms of their total line. The value of their property locally taxed in the state is of course deducted.

[3] 1898, 578, § 3.

[4] 1898, 578, § 4.

[5] 1898, 578, §§ 6-11. The commutation tax, including that for the Boston Elevated, is large. No exact data are given. From the data in the railroad commissioner's reports, on the basis of the amount paid by the larger companies, the tax would yield about $380,000 each year for 1904 and 1905.

gross receipts of its own or leased lines, if it declares no
dividends or if its dividends do not exceed six per cent.
Whenever dividends exceed this percentage, an additional
tax equal to the dividends in excess of six per cent becomes due.   This tax is distributed in the same way as
the tax on the corporate excess.[1]

Electric railroads constructed partly on private land
and partly on the public ways are, by an act of 1906, made
taxable like street railways. In the distribution of the tax,
however, only so much of the proceeds as corresponds to
the length of track in public ways is to be distributed to
the cities and towns, while the rest is to be distributed
like the tax on corporate excess.   The commutation tax
is levied only on so much of the line as is located in the
public ways.[2]   Street railways are further taxed, together
with railroads, on their gross receipts to maintain the
railroad commission.[3]

The law thus assigns to the cities and towns the
revenue derived from street railways.   It also makes
provision for a division of extraordinary profits between
the municipality and the corporation, seeking here to
secure a compensation for the special opportunity of
profit created by the community without suppressing the
motive for improvement.   In fact, however, this provision
is as yet merely on the statute book, no tax having been
paid under this clause.   A number of companies have
been paying eight per cent, and the Boston Elevated has
been paying six per cent.   The consolidation of strong
and weak companies would seem to leave open an avenue
of escape from this tax.[4]

[1] 1897, c. 500, § 10.   [2] 1906, c. 516, §§ 14-27.

[3] For a summary of the law and very much other information, see also
the *Census Special Report, Street and Electric Railways*, 1902.

[4] See Ripley, *op. cit.*, pp. 145-146.

To understand the significance of the taxation of street railways, we need consider therefore only the tax paid locally, and the tax on corporate excess, for the commutation tax may be regarded as a payment for special service. As already observed, but a small part of the taxes outside of the commutation tax is paid locally, that is, only about one-third.[1]

	Total Taxes.[2]	Com- mutation.	Local and Franchise.	Franchise.	Local.
1904	$1,761,000	$380,000	$1,381,000	$906,000	$475,000
1905	1,893,000	380,000	1,513,000	979,000	534,000

Since the tax is based on the capital stock, and since, in determining the valuation of the franchise, indebtedness is not considered, the result is that a very large part of the property of these corporations is exempted from taxation.[3] The bonds have a par value equal to nearly eighty per cent of the par value of the capital stock, and the increase of the proportion of bonded indebtedness since 1885 has been notable.[4]

[1] Statistical material, where no other source is assigned, is taken from data in the annual reports of the Railroad Commissioners.

[2] These figures probably include the railroad commissioners' tax, amounting, in 1904, to $9,429 and, in 1905, to $18,037. The figures for local and commutation taxes are estimated on the data for the larger companies, for which the commutation tax is separately reported.

[3] The Tax Commission of 1875 calls attention to the fact that as a result of the method of valuing the franchise, the rate of tax on property of street railways was about two-thirds of that on other property. *Report*, p. 128.

[4] The figures are as follows:

	Capital Stock.	Bonds.
1871	$5,051,000	$1,040,000
1885	8,077,000	3,455,000
1890	14,879,000	6,027,000
1895	27,906,000	22,284,000
1905	70,326,000	55,780,000

The total amount paid for interest on funded and unfunded debt amounted in 1904 to $2,670,000 and in 1905 to $2,897,000.

As the value of stocks in the more successful companies is very much above par, whereas bonds are apt to be nearer to par, the disproportion is not so great as is shown by this percentage, but it is none the less considerable. How important funded indebtedness is may be seen from the fact that, of the net income which is paid out, interest on the funded debt amounted in 1904 to $1,985,000 as compared with $3,214,000 paid in dividends. In 1905 the figures were respectively $2,278,000 and $3,556,000. Thus nearly forty per cent of the income paid out, or the property it represents, escapes taxation.[1] Moreover, as the proportion of bonds to capital stock is not the same either in market value or in amount outstanding, the effect must be inequality as between different street railways.[2]

As a result, the tax on street railways viewed as a property tax is both inadequate and inequitable.[·] Taking as a basis for property the data given in the reports of the railroad commissioners for construction, equipment, land and buildings, and other permanent assets,[3] the aver-

---

[1] See note 4, p. 117.

[2] Thus for 1905, in thousands of dollars:

	Capital.	Funded Debt.
Boston Elevated	13,300	7,500
Boston and Northern	10,360	9,659
Boston and Worcester	1,725	1,717
Holyoke	700	600
Old Colony	7,312	6,431
Springfield	1,958	1,500
Union	900	400
West End	16,089	15,977
Worcester	3,550	1,060

For the proportion of the total amount paid in interest and dividends going to each of the two items, see column V, in Appendix.

[·] This is of course the cost of construction, and therefore not a very satisfactory basis for the present value of the property. These items of

age tax rate for street railways amounted on this basis in 1904 to $10.66, and in 1905 to $11.23, or only about two-thirds of the average rate on property in the state. Considering only the eight leading companies—these together paid in 1905 $1,704,000 of the total taxes amounting to $1,893,000—the average rate per $1,000 for the period 1903–1905 is as follows:

Boston Elevated and West End	$18.68
Boston and Northern	6.35
Boston and Worcester	5.73
Holyoke	12.39
Old Colony	6.87
Springfield	14.32
Union	16.80
Worcester	12.65

Thus owing to the fact that the tax is computed on the basis of the market value of stock alone, the tax does not adequately reach property. Only in the case of the Boston Elevated is the rate greater than the tax rate on property; in the case of other companies it varies, and for most companies the rate is far below the rate on the general property.

We consider next the tax from the point of view of the income of the street railways. As a tax on the total receipts from operation, which are almost equivalent to the gross receipts from all sources,[1] the rate for all the street railways in the state was 5.27 per cent in 1904, and

intangible property amounted in 1905 to $134,698,000, while the gross assets aggregated $151,742,000. The tax rate on property in the state averaged $16.19 in 1904 and $16.83 in 1905; the rate on corporate excess was respectively $16.60 and $17.25.

[1] The other item, miscellaneous income, is equal to less than one per cent of the total earnings from operation, and to from two to three per cent of the net earnings from operation. Taxes are not included here in operating expenses.

5.58 per cent in 1905. Deducting operating expenses, the tax formed in 1904, 17.68 per cent and in 1905 17.24 per cent of the net receipts from operation. On the basis neither of gross receipts nor of net receipts does the tax operate uniformly. Thus for the three years 1903–1905, the Boston Elevated paid on the average 6.93 per cent of its total receipts from operation and the Union Street Railway Company paid 7.02 per cent; the Old Colony Company, on the other hand, paid 4.07 per cent and the Boston and Northern 3.51 per cent. Similar differences exist, if we take the percentage of net receipts from operation. The Boston Elevated paid 22.29 per cent, the Union Company and the Springfield Company each paid almost 20 per cent; on the other hand, the Old Colony paid 12.87 per cent, and the Boston and Northern and the Boston and Worcester each paid 10 per cent.

It is to be further noted that the companies paying the smallest percentage in taxes, are the companies which have a rather large funded debt. Thus it is again evident that the exemption of the debt in determining the taxable valuation results not only in inadequate, but also in unequal taxation as between the various companies. A tax levied on a valuation of both stocks and bonds would therefore yield a greater revenue, and, at the same time would tend to equalize taxation as between the companies.

Inasmuch as it has been urged of late in several quarters, notably by the recent Ontario Commission on Railway Taxation and the California Commission on Revenue and Taxation, that the taxation of gross receipts is the best mode of levying taxes on public-service corporations, it is of interest to observe that while a tax on gross receipts would involve some inequalities, these would not be so great as the inequalities involved in the present method of taxation. For, while the relation of gross receipts to net receipts is not constant, it is true that in case of the most important companies the rate of net to gross receipts does not seem to deviate much from the average for the state. The levy of a tax on gross receipts at the average per cent which is now paid by street railways in the state, would increase the total tax for most companies, in some instances as much as fifty per cent or even more, while on the other hand, in the case of a few companies, including however the Boston Elevated which pays one-half of the total taxes, it would reduce the tax by about twenty per cent. To levy the tax at the average rate of net receipts now taken by taxation, would give a different result in the case of some companies, whose operating expense is below the average, and increase their tax in several instances very considerably. The details may be gathered from a table in the Appendix.[1]

Summarizing, it may be said that the taxes paid by the street railways, exclusive of the commutation tax, amount to about five per cent of their gross receipts and about seventeen per cent of their net earnings. The total amount paid, including the commutation tax, aggregates nearly seven per cent of the gross income, and more than twenty per cent of the net income. Disregarding this tax for service, it appears that, except in the case of the Boston Elevated, the tax does not reach all tangible property, falling far below the rate levied on property, in the case of most companies. Street railways, it would thus seem, are not taxed more heavily than corporations generally, but on the contrary even more leniently.

The tax viewed in its relation to gross and net revenue

---

[1] See Appendix.

is objectionable as an unequal tax, imposing on some companies a burden which is twice as great as that imposed on other companies. The root of this evil is of course the inadequate basis of the tax, which allows property represented by indebtedness, or the income going to the bondholder to escape. Here obviously the reform, in keeping with present mode of utilizing market valuation, would be to adopt as the basis for taxation the value of both stocks and bonds. A departure from this system to the taxation of earnings would be, at least, more satisfactory than the present method of taxing street railways. With the careful supervision exercised by Massachusetts over her public-service corporations, a tax even on net earnings might be practicable.[1]

IV. *Railroads.*—In the taxation of railroads, one of the important features to note is that railroads are largely exempt from local taxation for their real estate as well as other tangible property. By court decision,[2] their road bed for a strip five rods in width, and their buildings erected within this area for railroad uses are exempt from taxation directly. Such real estate, together with their personal property, can be taxed only through the tax on corporate excess. Real estate outside of this limit is taxable, and an increasing proportion of the real estate of railroads is thus taxed locally, amounting in 1906 to $93,120,000, or a sum nearly equal to the

[1] In addition to references already cited, see also the following pamphlets: E. W. Burdett, *Argument for the Massachusetts Street Railway Association*, Boston, 1897; S. J. Elder, *Special Taxation for the Use of Streets*, Boston, 1897; J. P. Proctor, *Additional Burdens upon Street Railway Companies*, Boston, 1891; Whitney and Cummings. *Additional Burdens upon Street Railway Companies*, Boston, 1891. See also W. S. Allen, "Street Railway Franchises in Massachusetts," in *Annals of the Am. Acad. of Pol. and Soc. Science*, xxvii, pp. 101, 102.

[2] 4 Met. 564.

entire corporate excess ($95,000,000) on which the railroads are taxed by the state commissioner.[1]

Another, and very important, consideration for the taxation of railroads is the fact that in case of the railroads, as in the case of the street railways, bonds represent a very large proportion[2] of the total value of the companies operating in Massachusetts, as may be seen from the following table:[3]

	Capital Stock.	Bonds.
1871	$75,202,000	$16,847,000
1880	118,738,000	60,813,000
1890	157,243,000	102,718,000
1905	238,223,000	159,098,000

Bonds at par thus represent a sum equal to two-thirds of the par value of the railroad stocks. In fact, however, the value of the capital stock represents a greater percentage of the value of the railroads, than is shown by the above figures, for some railroad stocks have a market value more than double their par value, whereas bonds are nearer to par. Nevertheless the value of the capital stock alone remains an inadequate basis for the taxation of either railroad property or railroad income. Furthermore, in view of the varying proportion of stocks

---

[1] In 1873 the valuation of corporate excess was $42,982,000, while the valuation of property was only $22,127,000. See *Report of the Tax Commission*, 1875, p. 174.

[2] For the more important leased lines for which the tax is given in the *Auditor's Report*, the relation of bonds to capital stock is as follows:

	Capital.	Funded Debt.
Boston and Albany	$25,000,000	$8,485,000
Boston and Lowell	6,599,000	8,528,000
Boston and Maine	17,787,000	30,808,000
Fitchburg	24,360,000	22,174,000
Old Colony	17,880,000	15,511,000

[3] See data in *Reports of the Railroad Commissioners*.

and bonds outstanding for different roads, the tax can not be equitable.[1]

The tax commission of 1875, estimating the value of railroad property to be the cost of construction, found that the railroads were thus taxed at only about two-thirds of the rate which they would pay on property. The commission however contented itself with the suggestion that a better method of valuing the franchise be found, which would compel railroad property to contribute its full share.[2]   A committee of the State Railroad Commissioners, of which C. F. Adams, one of the Massachusetts railroad commissioners, was a member, condemned in their report the Massachusetts system as being based upon no recognized principle, allowing a heavily bonded road practically to escape taxation, as fluctuating widely in amount, and imposing a burden, which owing to disregard of debt in taxation, had no necessary relation to actual earning capacity whether net or gross.[3] Although these obvious defects of the tax have been perceived long ago, not until recently have measures been presented in the legislature to remedy them.[4]

[1] As early as 1843 a special tax on railroads was proposed (1843 *House Doc.* 92).   In advance of the general corporation tax it was proposed in 1860 to tax railroads on the value of so much of their capital as had been expended in Massachusetts, and divide the income between the towns through which the railroads passed, and the towns in which the shareholders resided (1860 *House Doc.* 153).   In 1870 when the federal tax on gross receipts had been removed, it was proposed to levy a similar state tax. The legislative committee to whom the measure was referred condemned it as utterly inexpedient, an attempt to conceal the extent of the burden laid on the people by making the common carriers tax collectors.   Such a tax, the committee feared, would prevent the reduction of rates (1878 *House Doc.* 287).

[2] *Report*, pp. 127, 128, 174, 175.

[3] C. F. Adams, W. B. Williams and J. H. Oberly, *Taxation of Railroads and Railroad Securities*, 1880, pp. 7, 8.

[4] See *e. g.*, 1902, *House Doc.* 895; 1904, *House Doc.* 581; 1906, *House Doc.* 713, and *Report of the Special Joint Committee on Taxation*, 1907, pp. 33–35.

For interstate roads the basis of taxation is a fraction of the capital stock equal to the proportion of the total line which is located in the state. In view of the density of population, and the industrial character of the state, this method of determining the amount on which railroads are to be taxed in the state is certainly not unduly favorable to Massachusetts. The joint special tax committee of 1894 thought that the proportion of total track mileage instead of line mileage would give the state a fairer basis for the tax,[1] but this suggestion was not adopted, and the practical difference would not be great. A better basis would be the proportion of gross receipts received in Massachusetts.[2]

Railroads are thus taxed[3] by a system in which a state official coöperates with local officers. The local assessors tax part of the real estate and machinery where there is any. The tax commissioner further assesses the railroads on the proportion of the market value of their capital stock corresponding to the length of line in Massachusetts. From this sum the value of the property taxed locally, that is, so much of their real estate as is not exempt and their machinery in the state, is deducted. More than one-half of the taxes paid by the railroads are paid as a tax on the corporate excess. This may be seen from the following table:

[1] *Report*, pp. 29, 30. Thus for 1905 the total length of road and branches of railroads operating in Massachusetts is given as 3,787 miles; the length in Massachusetts is 2,105 miles. The total length of single track is given as 7,654 miles; for Massachusetts the length is 4,490 miles.

[2] See B. H. Meyer, "Methods for the Distribution of Railway Values among the States," in the *Census Bulletin*, no. 21, *Commercial Valuation of Railway Operating Property in the United States*, 1904, pp. 51, 52.

[3] 1906, c. 463, pt. ii, §§ 211–217.

TAXES ON RAILROADS

	Total Taxes.[1]	Per Mile.	On Real and Personal Estate.	On Capital.	Miscellaneous.
1901....	$2,925,598	$1,401	$1,013,313	$1,667,219	$244,974
1902....	2,957,581	1,413	1,153,358	1,658,385	165,838
1903....	2,981,157	1,426	1,234,470	1,589,497	157,190
1904....	3,070,766	1,472	1,404,382	1,482,504	183,880

In 1906 the railroads paid a franchise tax on $95,000,000, and a tax locally on real estate and machinery valued at $93,120,000; it thus appears that an increasing proportion of the total tax is paid on property reached by the local assessors. In addition to their local taxes and the tax on corporate excess, the railroads, together with the street railways, are assessed on their gross receipts in order to defray the cost of maintaining the board of railroad commissioners. The tax assessed for this purpose on railroads amounted, in 1905, to $32,245.

Data are not available for determining the significance of the taxes in Massachusetts from the point of view of either gross or net income. As, however, the method of taxing railroads is in the main the same as that employed in the taxation of street railways, the same criticisms as to the inadequacy of the basis for valuation, and the inequality involved in it would apply also to the railroads. The Census Bulletin on the commercial valuation of railway operating property gives $250,052,-000 as the commercial value of the railway operating property of Massachusetts in 1904.[1] The property as-

---

The taxes as reported in the *Statistics of Railways* are for the year ending in June. For Massachusetts they correspond to the taxes for the year previous, and the dates have been given accordingly.

[1] See *Census Bulletin*, no. 21, *Commercial Valuation of Railway Operating Property*, p. 8. With reference to taxation, Professor Adams says of this valuation that while it would be too high as a valuation of the physical elements, " if, on the other hand, it is the purpose of the taxing law to appraise railway property at its true cash value, unusual or

sessed locally to the railways in Massachusetts amounted in 1906 to $93,120,000; the corporate excess to about $95,000,000.[1] That is to say the railroads are taxed on less than $200,000,000, so that on the basis of the census calculations the railroads escape taxes in Massachusetts on about one-fourth of the commercial value of their operating property.

Nevertheless railroads pay in Massachusetts a higher tax per mile than in any other state in the Union. For 1904 the taxes per mile, as reported in the statistics of the Interstate Commerce Commission, amounted to $1,472. Disregarding the District of Columbia, which received $1,349 per mile, Connecticut, in which the railroads are taxed on the market valuation of both stocks and bonds, comes next with $1,259 per mile, but the tax rate in Connecticut is one per cent, whereas in Massachusetts it is between one and one-half and one and three-quarters per cent.[2] On the other hand, the value of railroads in Massachusetts per mile, $118,000, is exceeded in Pennsylvania, Rhode Island, New Jersey and the District of Columbia. Massachusetts thus derives a greater revenue in proportion to her mileage from the railroads than any other state.[3]

The method employed in taxing railways has at least

abnormal conditions being excluded, it may be that the commercial valuation of operating property submitted in this report fairly measures its appraisal for the purpose of taxation." *Ibid.*, p. 9.

[1] For these figures, see *Report of Joint Special Committee on Taxation*, pp. 36 and 132. The tax on corporate excess for 1906, at the rate of $16.87, is $1,597,063, which would mean a corporate excess of $94,668,900.

[2] The other states receiving a high tax per mile are Rhode Island $1,049, New Jersey $848, New York $617, and Ohio $478. See *Statistics of Railways in the United States*, 1905, p. 100.

[3] See *Census Bulletin*, no. 21, p. 8.

the advantage of simplicity.   The stock market furnishes the data, and the quotations for the first of May are taken, instead of any average.[1]   Bonds are left to the general property tax, which means that in general they escape taxation.   The railroads are satisfied, and make no complaint of the present system, whereas, they naturally oppose the addition of bonds to capital stock in determining the taxable value of railroads.

The distribution of the proceeds of the tax on the corporate excess of railroads has been a special cause for grievance, owing to the fact that in the case of railroads the value of their corporate excess represents a large amount of real estate that is exempt from local taxation.   Hence the demand for a change by which the revenue will accrue in a greater measure to the communities through which the railroad passes, or be retained by the state.   The latter plan was advocated by the recent special tax committee.   In view of the general rather than local field of the railways, such a disposition of the revenue would seem best.   Here, of course, the local self-interest of the towns that profit by the present distribution of the proceeds stands in the way of reform.[2]

Massachusetts has been backward in the taxation of other transportation agencies connected with the railways.   Neither express companies, nor sleeping or dining car or special service freight car companies, have been subjected to taxation.   The excise tax on foreign

[1] See interview with the tax commissioner, Mr. Trefry, in the *Report of the Ontario Commission*, p. 122.

[2] For a general account and criticism of the Massachusetts system of taxing railways, see also *Report of the California Commission on Revenue and Taxation*, 1906, particularly pp. 111–115, and the *Report of the Ontario Commission on the Taxation of Railways*, 1905, particularly pp. 117–122.

corporations is the only tax to which such companies are now subject, except for property that is reached by the local authorities. As these corporations have little property subject to local taxation and the excise tax is fixed at a maximum of $2,000, there is no provision for taxing such corporation adequately. Moreover, the larger express companies are organized as voluntary associations, and, as such, are not liable to taxation as corporations.[1]

The special committee on taxation of 1907, proposed a tax on express companies[2] on the market value of their stocks and bonds after deducting the value of locally taxed property. The proportion of their gross receipts in Massachusetts to their total gross receipts is suggested as the proportion of the market value of their securities on which to assess the tax. A similar provision ought to be made for the taxation of all special service car companies.[3]

V. *Gas and Electric Companies.*—Gas and electric companies differ from other public-service corporations in that they have been treated as manufacturing companies, and therefore made taxable on their equipment in the streets as on machinery.[4] The result, at least so far as gas companies are concerned, is that by far the greater part of their taxes are paid locally, and only a small part, as a tax on their corporate excess. Moreover, in the case of both of these classes of corporations the proportion of bonded indebtedness to capital stock is smaller than in the case of the public-service corporations already considered. Their taxes would therefore

---

[1] *Report*, pp. 2, 35–39.   [2] *Ibid.*, pp. 39–41.

[3] See also 1904, *House Doc.*, no. 956.

[4] 12 Allen 75. See also 1902, c. 342. They are not, however, under the business corporation tax.

be assessed on a fuller valuation of the income-bearing property than is the case with other public-service corporations.

For gas companies the relation of capital stock to indebtedness, and the local valuation of property is as follows : [1]

	1890.	1904.
Capital	$13,158,000	$27,783,000
Bonds	449,000	1,314,000
Notes payable	554,000	2,847,000
Valuation	14,615,000	30,225,000
Taxes	269,000	507,000

On the basis of the local valuation the total taxes for the period 1900–1904, indicate that gas companies paid a rate a little in excess of both the average tax rate on property in the state, and of the rate of tax on the corporate excess.   For 1904 they paid taxes at the rate of $16.77, whereas the average rate on property was $16.19, and on corporate excess $16.60.[2]   Of their total taxes for 1904, amounting to $507,170, gas companies paid on corporate excess $59,379, to which is to be added part of $23,438 paid by gas and electric companies.   Gas companies thus pay nearly all of their taxes directly to the cities and towns in which their works are located.

On the basis of their earnings the taxes paid by gas companies, for the period 1900–1904, amount to about five per cent of the gross receipts.   The municipality and state thus receive about five cents for every thousand feet of gas used by the consumer.   Deducting operating expenses from the gross receipts and using the result as

[1] All statistical data are taken from the annual reports of the *Gas and Electric Light Commission*, where no other source is assigned.

[2] For 1900–1904 gas companies paid at an average rate of $17.31, whereas the rate on property for the state for this period was $15.94, and on corporate excess $16.43.

a basis for net receipts, the taxes would be equal to about fifteen per cent.[1] As no allowance is here made for depreciation and other items, taxes in reality form a larger proportion of net receipts.[2]

Electric companies differ from gas companies in several respects. Their indebtedness as compared with their capital stock is greater than in the case of gas companies, as is shown by the following table:

	1901.	1905.
Capital	$12,764,000	$18,333,000
Bonds	3,615,000	3,107,000
Notes payable	2,965,000	3,130,000

The local valuation of property in 1904, was $20,040,-000, the total taxes were $598,035. The tax rate would be $29.84, which is very much in excess of the rate on the property taxable locally.[3] Consequently in the case

---

[1] The relation of taxes to earnings is as follows:

	Per cent of gross income.	Per cent of income from sale of gas.	Per cent of gross income minus operating expenses.	Amount per 1000 feet.
1900	5.27	5.4	14.60	.05
1901	4.88	5.1	13.18	.047
1902	4.50	4.3	13.16	.043
1903	4.84	4.9	14.82	.047
1904	4.86	5.1	13.42	.049

[2] See A. E. Pillsbury, *Argument for the Association of Massachusetts Gas Companies*, etc., Boston, 1903.

[3] For individual companies the rate of taxes on the basis of the local valuation as compared with the local rate on property for 1903 and 1904, indicates that these companies pay more than a tax on tangible property. Thus the Edison Company (Boston) paid on the basis of its valuation at the rate of $26.52 in 1903 and $29.39 in 1904, whereas the property rate was respectively $14.80 and $15.20. The Lowell Company paid $30.99 in 1904 when the local rate was $20.00. On the other hand, for some cities the difference is not so marked, the Cambridge Company paying $19.74 when the local rate was $17.90; the Worcester Company $19.74 as against a local rate of $17.40.

of electric companies, about one-third of the total taxes are paid on the corporate excess, electric companies paying $193,091 and part of the $23,438 paid by gas and electric companies.

From the point of view of income,[1] the taxes form between six and seven per cent of the gross income and about fourteen per cent of the net receipts. The taxes[2] on electric companies, it appears, mean more than a tax on tangible property, the corporation tax serving here to reach some of the earning power due to special opportunity.

VI. *Telegraph and Telephone Companies.*—Telegraph and telephone companies are taxed under the general corporation tax. Interstate telegraph companies, like railroads, are taxed on the proportion of the market value of their capital stock which corresponds to the part of their line in Massachusetts; the tax commissioner assesses the corporation tax on this amount, making deduction, however, for the value of property locally taxed, namely, real estate and machinery, and, since 1902, also conduits and wires.

[1] The relation of taxes to the income of the electric light companies is given in the following table of percentages:

	Gross income.	Income from sale of electricity.	Net income deducting amount for depreciation.
1900	4.59	4.84	11.3
1901	5.94	6.32	13.8
1902	5.62	5.82	14.5
1903	6.41	6.82	13.6
1904	7.17	7.37	15.5

[2] In addition to the ordinary property and franchise taxes, gas and electric companies are taxed on their gross receipts to defray the cost of maintaining the board of gas and electric commissioners and also of inspection. The sum assessed for the former purpose amounted in 1905 to $19,579. Inspection fees amounted to $13,341. *R. L.*, c. 121, §§ 4, 36, 37.

Telephone companies were not given special attention in the tax laws until 1885.[1] For interstate telephone companies the proportion of the total number of telephones used in the state was then made the measure of the proportion of the capital stock on which telephone companies are liable to taxation. Companies organized in Massachusetts, moreover, are allowed for taxation the privilege of deducting from the value of their capital stock the value of all stocks in other corporations held by them on which the tax has been actually paid.[2] This measure was intended to facilitate the holding of stocks in Massachusetts and foreign companies. In spite of this concession, however, the Bell Telephone Company which had paid in 1899 $506,607, or more than the total now received from all telephone and telegraph companies, transferred its property to a New York corporation, the American Telephone and Telegraph Company, thereby lightening its tax burden considerably.[3]

In 1894 the special tax committee proposed to change the basis for determining the proportion of capital to be taxed in Massachusetts from the length of line to the number of miles of wire.[4] In the agitation for imposing a special franchise tax on public-service corporations, the telephone and telegraph companies have been included, but no change in the manner of taxing these corporations or of distributing the revenue has as yet been made, other than that of taxing the wires and conduits locally. The recent special tax committee proposed, however, that the state retain the revenue from telegraph and telephone companies, as well as that from railroads.[5]

[1] 1885, c. 238, § 1.   [2] 1886, c. 227, § 1.

[3] J. M. Hallowell, "The Corporation Franchise Tax," *Review and Record*, Sept. 17, 1904. (Reprint, p. 8.)

[4] *Report*, pp. 29, 30.   [5] *Report*, p. 35.

In the case of telephone and telegraph companies the tax paid on corporate excess is far greater than the tax paid on property assessed locally. Thus the value of the property locally assessed in 1906 amounted to $10,176,-937, on which the tax would be about $170,000. The tax on the corporate excess, on the other hand, amounted for the same year to $466,278, the greater part of which is retained by the state.[1] For telegraph and telephone companies the valuation of capital stock alone must be an unsatisfactory basis for taxation. Of the two most important companies, which alone pay ninety per cent of the tax, the American Telephone and Telegraph Company has a capital stock outstanding of $99,008,000, and a bonded debt of $38,000,000, whereas for the New England Telephone and Telegraph Company the figures are respectively $21,616,000 and $4,000,000.[2] For the telephone business the total revenue is given for 1902 as $6,127,452, and the total taxes as $366,879, or nearly six per cent of the gross revenue.[3] Deducting therefrom the operating expense, the tax on the net receipts amounts to nineteen per cent.

From the point of view of revenue, by far the greatest proportion comes from telephone companies. The income from this class of corporations increased very rapidly after 1885, reaching $159,441 in 1890, and $211,-010 in 1891. Nearly the entire tax paid in 1905 by telephone and telegraph companies, amounting in all to $486,489, is paid by three companies, the American Telephone and Telegraph Company, $160,465; the New

[1] *Report*, p. 36.

[2] *Census Special Report, Telephones and Telegraphs*, 1902, p. 13.

[3] *Ibid.*, p. 83. Aside from the information in the *Census Special Report*, there are no data available to indicate the significance of the tax for telephone and telegraph companies.

England Telephone and Telegraph Company, $310,861, and the Western Union Telegraph Company, $11,366.

Of the other important public-service corporations steamboats are taxed under the general corporation tax, and there are no special features involved. Water companies have never been of much importance from the point of view of the revenue collected by the state, and the amount they pay on corporate excess is declining.[1]

In conclusion we call attention to the significance of the taxes on public-service corporations for the public. We have seen that in the case of the street railways, the gas and electric companies, and the telephone companies, about five per cent of the gross receipts is paid to the state and municipalities, and a similar proportion probably obtains for the other corporations. Out of every dollar paid by the consumer for the services of these public-utility companies, five cents is contributed to the government.

[1] In 1902 their pipes and conduits in the streets, which have been declared exempt from local taxation by court decision (100 Mass. 183), were made taxable *in situ* (c. 342), and their real estate had been so taxed by custom, so that most of their property was reached by the local assessors. A recent decision, however, exempts these companies from local taxation on their real estate which has been acquired by eminent domain or might have been so acquired. This would of course mean that water companies would pay a greater part of their taxes on corporate excess. The recent tax committee recommends, therefore, legislation to restore the former practice. Milford Water Co. *vs.* Town of Hopkinton (July 14, 1906). See *Report of the Joint Special Committee on Taxation*, p. 42; and C. J. Bullock, *Quarterly Journal of Economics*, Feb., 1907, pp. 216, 217.

CHAPTER VI

Taxation of Financial Corporations

In taxing financial corporations, a distinction is made between companies carrying on their business for private profit and mutual corporations. Under the first head come trust companies, stock insurance companies, and banks. Trust companies and stock insurance companies are taxed under the general corporation tax, and banks, although excepted from this general law on account of their federal charter, are taxed in a similar way.

Mutual corporations, on the other hand, are regarded as trustees for the public, and their activity is deemed worthy of special encouragement. Hence savings banks and mutual insurance companies are favored in the rate at which they are taxed. In the absence of capital stock, the measure of the tax is, in general, the amount of business. Thus for savings banks the average amount of deposits, and for insurance companies, other than life insurance companies, the amount of premiums received in the state—is the basis for assessment. For life insurance companies, however, the tax is assessed on the net value of policies held by Massachusetts citizens. As evidence of a plan of encouragement, it is further to be noted that, while corporations having a capital stock were always taxed in the state, either directly or indirectly, the systematic taxation of mutual corporations, like savings banks and insurance companies, dates only from the war, and life insurance was not subjected to taxation until 1880.

We turn to a more detailed consideration of the taxation of financial institutions, taking up first trust companies and banks. Although stock insurance companies are taxed like these institutions, we shall consider these insurance companies later, in connection with insurance companies generally.

I. *Trust Companies.*—As trust companies were incorporated they were treated for taxation like other corporations having a capital stock. At the same time use was made of them for taxing the personal property which they held in trust and, subsequently, also the deposits in their keeping. These companies are required to pay a tax at the same rate as on their corporate excess on personal property held in trust by them, which would be taxable to an individual trustee. The revenue from this source is distributed in the same way as the tax on shares, that is the state retains so much as is paid on the property of non-residents, and distributes the remainder to the cities and towns in which the beneficiaries of these trust funds reside. Money, which is not held in trust, but which is deposited on interest or for investment, is taxed at a rate equivalent to three-fourths of the rate on corporate excess. As the rate on corporate excess is generally higher than one and one-half per cent, the rate on deposits would thus exceed one per cent. Deposits which can be withdrawn on demand or on ten days notice are, however, exempt. Trust companies are thus taxed on their capital stock directly. They are also used to collect a tax on trust property and on time deposits held by them.[1]

[1] This method of taxing trust companies was fully developed in 1873

With regard to the taxation of trust companies on their capital stock, the feature to which attention is to be called is the method by which the tax can be largely reduced.[1]   Under the Massachusetts law, mortgages are regarded as an interest in real estate.   By court decision deduction is, therefore, to be made for mortgages in determining the corporate excess.[2]   While all corporations are entitled to this deduction, trust companies can take special advantage of it, for among their assets are loans on real estate, constituting an amount equal to more than one-third of their capital stock.[3]   The extent to which the tax can be reduced on account of this exemption is very considerable, and in some instances the entire tax on the corporate excess of the trust companies can be evaded.[4]

When mortgages were made an interest in real estate, the contemplation of the law was that the holder of the mortgage should pay the tax on so much of the real estate as was represented by the value of the mortgage.

(see 1873, c. 285, §§ 8, 9, and 1888, c. 413, §§ 21–23).   For earlier trust companies the method of reaching trust property was different.   At first they were required only to make returns to the tax commissioner of this property, and the tax commissioner notified in turn the local assessors.   (See 1869, c. 296, § 6; 1870, c. 323, §§ 4, 5.)   In 1871 the present method was adopted (1871, c. 142, § 3, and subsequent acts).   In 1873 the tax on deposits was added.

[1] For this aspect of the taxation of trust companies, as also for the other features of the working of the tax on trust companies, see the discussion of Professor Bullock, in his article "The Taxation of Corporations in Massachusetts," *Quarterly Journal of Economics*, xxi, 222–225.

[2] 137 Mass. 80.

[3] For 1905 the capital stock is $17,076,000; loans on real estate amount to $6,149,000.   See *Report of the Board of Commissioners of Savings Banks* for 1905, pt. i, p. 817.

[4] For a number of trust companies no tax on corporate excess is reported by the auditor.

In practice, however, the law means that a mortgage loan on real estate is exempt from taxation, and that the borrower pays the tax on all his real estate. In taxing trust companies on the market value of their shares, the intent of the law is obviously here as elsewhere to use the value of the capital stock as a measure of their tax-paying ability. Deduction is made for real estate to avoid double taxation. But there is no reason for deducting the value of mortgage loans, because in practice these are not taxed. Moreover, the mortgages for which deduction can be demanded, may be bought with depositors' money, and thus used merely as a means of escaping the tax.[1]

The revenue from the tax on deposits and on property held in trust is very small, and moreover has been declining. The tax on personal property has naturally driven trust companies to place their investments in forms of personalty which are exempt from taxation to the holder in Massachusetts. Thus of the $26,419,000 of property reported as held in the trust departments of these corporations, mortgages on Massachusetts real estate ($8,738,000) stocks of New England railroads ($6,382,000) and real estate (2,762,000) alone constitute more than two-thirds.[2] For property held in trust these companies are in law taxable as individual trus-

---

[1] Savings banks are exempt on the mortgages held by them. But the reason for this exemption is of a different character. Mortgages constitute, as we shall see, their largest field of investment. A tax on deposits so invested, when individual lenders were exempt, would place them, it was feared, at a disadvantage in making loans on real estate.

[2] See data in *Report of Commissioners of Savings Banks* for 1905, i, p. 817. It is to be noted that the report here is for Oct. 31, 1905, whereas property held in trust, like all property, is taxable as it stands on May first. It would thus be possible to evade the law by substituting on the date of assessment non-taxable securities, a device used by individual trustees.

tees. Only two companies, however, paid a tax in 1905 upon such property, and they contributed but $8,004.[1] This would seem to indicate evasion. For the same year railroad bonds alone, which are taxable, are reported as held by the trust department to the amount of $1,062,000.[2] On this item alone the tax would have been more than double this amount.

The tax on money deposited on interest and time deposits in trust companies is very heavy as compared with the tax on deposits in savings banks. Whereas for deposits in savings banks the rate is one-half per cent, and in fact, only about one-fourth per cent, the rate on deposits in trust companies would be about one and one-quarter per cent. For 1904 and 1905 time deposits are reported by the commissioners of savings banks separately, as of October thirty-first. The figures are respectively $6,072,000 and $6,079,000.[3] Only four companies in 1905 paid a tax on deposits, in the aggregate only $898,[4] which at the tax rate for 1905 would indicate deposits amounting to less than $70,000. It would seem to be a better policy to tax trust companies for their deposits not as they stand on the first of May, but on the average amount, as is done in the case of the savings banks.

The amount of personal property and deposits reached through trust companies, and the tax collected, as reported by the tax commissioner, showed a notable decline. In 1893 the figures were $1,339,000, in 1895, $1,235,000, in 1900, $1,150,000 in 1904, $894,000 and in 1905, $504,000. For

---

[1] See Bullock, *op. cit.,* p. 225.

[2] *Report of Commissioners of Savings Banks* for 1905, i, p. 817.

[3] See *Reports of the Commissioners of Savings Banks.* Prof. Bullock notes that in one case $2,000,000 reported as time deposits was virtually subject to withdrawal at short notice. *Op. cit.,* p. 225.

[4] Bullock, *op. cit.,* p. 225.

1906 there is a gain, $812,000 being reported. The taxes have sunk from $20,000 in 1893, to $8,000 in 1905. For 1906 the tax is $13,000. On the other hand, the funds held in the trust departments do not show such a decline, rising on the contrary, from $13,875,000 in 1900 to $25,419,000 in 1905. It may be that the weight of the tax has restricted trust companies mainly to a banking business, so that the holding of personal property in trust has been left largely in the hands of individual trustees, and the holding of deposits is restricted to savings banks.

The tax paid by trust companies, as reported by the auditor, shows a rapid growth, reflecting the growth of these companies, and rises from $4,000 in 1871 to $478,000 in 1905. These figures include, it seems, not only the tax on corporate excess but also the taxes on trust property and deposits. Adding to the tax on corporate excess for 1905 the tax on the real estate of trust companies, which would amount to about $70,000 (assuming the same rate as that paid on corporate excess) the total taxes of these corporations would amount to about $550,000. This would be equivalent to a tax at the rate of $15.00 per thousand on the total amount of their capital stock and surplus fund; [1] a rate somewhat less than the average rate on property.

II. *Taxation of Banks.*—Banks are taxed, not under the general corporation tax, but with some modifications under the general property tax. Although the tax is levied on property, that is on the shares, and not on the franchise of the bank, it is in effect the same. For although the tax is

---

[1] For the leading trust companies the rate computed in this way varies widely. While in one instance it is $30.59 and in another $38.83, other companies pay variously $19.32, $17.24, $12.66, $18.63, $13.01, $18.05. The lowest rate is paid by a trust company more than one-half of the surplus and capital of which is invested in loans on real estate.

on the shares, it is collected from the banks and not from the shareholders.   In practice the tax is treated by the banks as an item of expense and deducted from the dividends.

Like other corporations, banks are taxed on their real estate, and on the market value of their shares in excess of their real estate.   The tax on this excess is assessed, however, by the local assessors instead of by the state tax commissioner.   Moreover banks are not assessed at one uniform rate throughout the state, but at the tax rate of the city or town in which they are located.   The proceeds are, in general, distributed like the yield of the tax on corporations.   Insurance companies and certain institutions and individuals exempt for their personal property under the general tax law, receive a refund of the tax on their shares. Part of the tax on shares owned by saving banks is similarly refunded to these institutions.   In consequence, a considerable deduction is made from the yield of the tax on banks before it becomes part of the state and local revenue.

The banks thus taxed are all national banks.   The state banks at the close of the war adopted federal charters, and the only banking institutions under state charter are the trust companies.   On account of their federal charter, national banks were excepted from the general corporation tax.   The assessment of shares to the owners, with all the administrative difficulties involved, continued therefore for nearly a decade, and not until many experiments had been tried, was the present system adopted in 1873.

The obstacle in the way of a simple centralized administration was presented, in the first place, by federal legislation.   Under the act of 1864,[1] the supreme court of the state held that Congress had not authorized a tax on all the shares of the bank collectively, or on shareholders over

---

[1] *U. S. Statutes at Large*, vol. 13, p. 111.

whom the state had no jurisdiction.[1]   No attempt was
made, therefore, to tax non-residents for their shares, and
Massachusetts citizens were taxed for bank shares by the
local assessors where they resided.[2]

In 1868 Congress defined more clearly the restrictions it
had imposed on the taxation of bank shares.   It permitted
the state to determine the manner and place of taxing all
shares of national banking associations located within its
jurisdiction, subject however to two restrictions, namely,
that the tax on shares was not to be at a greater rate than
on other moneyed capital, and that the shares of non-residents were to be taxed in no place other than where the bank
was located.[3]   The legislature took advantage of this act at
first only for taxing the shares of non-residents.[4]   In accordance with the federal law these were taxed in the place
where the bank was located.   The rate was made the tax
rate of the particular city or town and the proceeds were
remitted to the state treasury.[5]

This method was unsatisfactory, as it still left the shares
of resident stockholders taxable to each of them according
to his place of residence, and thus introduced a variety of
rates for shares in the same bank.   Furthermore, this
method allowed also of much evasion.[6]   In 1871 it was,
therefore, provided that all shares in a bank be assessed in

[1] 14 Allen, 359, 99 Mass., 141 ; 1868, House Doc., no. 348.

[2] 1865, c. 242. See also 1867, c. 188.

[3] *U. S. Revised Statutes,* 5219.

[4] These, according to incomplete returns, had a market value in
1868 of $11,990,438.38, on which the tax would have been $151,639.65,
a very considerable sum. *Treasurer's Report* for 1869, pp. 7-8, and
for 1868, p. 19.

[5] 1868, c. 349, 101 Mass., 575 ; 104 Mass., 586.

[6] 1871 *Sen. Doc.,* 299, where the evasion is estimated to have been
as much as forty per cent.

the place where the bank is located.[1] The unwillingness of the banks to co-operate in the fuller taxation of bank stock, by paying the tax for shareholders, led to difficulties and complaint, and the law was repealed.[2] The benefits to both local and state treasuries from the more effective law had been very large.[3] The loss of revenue consequent upon the repeal[4] and the inconvenience attendant upon the decentralized administration led, therefore, in 1873 to the re-enactment of a law like that of 1871, according to which the banks are still taxed.[5] It was upheld by the courts and under it there were substantial gains in the revenue of both state and municipalities,—a testimony to the efficiency of a more centralized administration. The banks this time assumed the tax,[6] paying it as a current expense.[7]

The law taxing bank shares provides for the assessment of all the shares of a bank at their market value in the town or city in which the bank is located. From the value of the capital stock is deducted the value of the real estate locally taxed. The rate of taxation on the excess is the local rate. This rate is determined, however, by excluding from the local valuation the value of shares held by those who do not reside in the city or town. The tax is collected by the authorities of the locality in which the bank is situated. So much of the tax as is due on the shares of residents in the town or city is retained by them. The cities and towns are allowed one per cent for the expense of assessment and

[1] 1871, c. 390.   [2] 1872, c. 321.

[3] The tax commissioner estimated the total gain at $654,571. *Report for* 1871, p. 11.

[4] The income of the state from the bank tax fell from $311,312 to $137,386. *Report of the Tax Commissioner* for 1873, p. 11.

[5] 1873, c. 315; 125 U. S., 60; 175 Mass., 257.

[6] *Report of the Tax Commissioner* for 1874, p. 11.

[7] For a full discussion of the various changes in the law, and the effects, see *Report of the Tax Commission* of 1875, pp. 128-135.

collection. The remainder of the tax is remitted to the state treasury.

The tax commissioner apportions so much of the tax as corresponds to the shares owned by persons resident in the state to the cities and towns in which they live. The tax on shares owned outside of the state is retained in the treasury. So much as is due on the shares of insurance companies is returned to them. Up to 1881 the entire tax on shares owned by savings banks was refunded to them. Since that year, however, there is refunded to them instead a sum equal to the tax which they pay on deposits invested in bank shares.[1] The tax on shares owned by philanthropic and educational institutions is refunded. Moreover, persons exempt under the general property tax may secure from the cities and towns in which they live a return of the tax on shares owned by them.

In consequence of these numerous refunds the net revenue accruing to the state and to the cities and towns is much reduced, as may be seen from the following table: [2]

TAX ON BANKS.
(In thousands of dollars.)

	Total Amount.	Amount accruing to		Amount refunded to		
		Cities and Towns.	State Treasury.	Savings Banks.	Insurance Companies.	Societies, etc.
1871	$1,530	$946	$331	$252		
1873	1,544	975	207	319	$20	20
1880	1,652	1,003	193	390	40	23
1881	1,647	997	192	395	38	33
1882	1,721	1,033	491	126	41	28
1884	1,856	1,098	542	129	53	33
1890	1,693	987	488	140	39	32
1895	1,566	923	435	145	28	33
1900	1,475	907	405	110	18	33
1905	1,418	926	370	70	17	33

[1] 1881, c. 305, § 2. In effect, savings banks are not taxed for deposits invested in bank shares.

[2] For data see *Reports of the Tax Commissioner.*

Up to 1881 about twenty-five per cent of the total tax was refunded, most of this amount to savings banks. When, however, in 1881 savings banks were exempted for mortgages, the law was modified, so that these institutions no longer receive a refund of the entire tax on their shares. Only an amount equal to the tax which savings banks pay on deposits invested in bank stocks is refunded. This change resulted in doubling the income of the state from the bank tax. Whereas before that period the total amount of the tax refunded was twenty-seven per cent in 1880 and 1881, in 1882 the amount refunded fell to eleven per cent, and in 1905 it was only eight per cent.[1]

For state revenue the proportion yielded by the bank tax rose from over four per cent for 1871-1880 to nine per cent for 1881-1885. Since that period the bank tax as a source of income for both state and local bodies has steadily declined both absolutely and relatively.[2] This decline is due to the decrease of bank capital.[3] For the five year period 1901-1905 only four per cent of the revenue of the state was derived from this source.

As in the case of the general corporation tax, the greater part of the yield of the bank tax accrues to the municipalities, more than two-thirds being distributed among the cities and towns. Likewise the distribution of this tax on banks results in a similar concentration of the proceeds in the residential towns. The same criticism is applicable here as in

---

[1] It will be noted that the exemption of banks shares to insurance companies and savings banks led to larger holdings of these securities, as is shown by the increase in the amount refunded to these institutions. This feature of the law evoked criticism from the tax commission of 1875. *Report*, p. 71.

[2] See p. 37 *supra*.

[3] Thus the bank capital for Massachusetts as reported by the comptroller was $96,667,000 in 1890, $78,392,000 in 1901, and $64,017,000 in 1905.

the case of the distribution of the corporation tax. Another criticism of the bank tax pertains to the varying rate at which it is assessed, the local rate of the town in which the tax is located being the rate of tax on banks. This, it seems, can not be avoided under existing federal legislation. While, on the one hand, this feature of the law results in an inequality of tax rate among banks, there is, on the other hand, an advantage in the tax rate to most holders of bank stock, for nearly one half of the bank capital is assessed in Boston, which enjoys a lower rate than the average rate in the state.

Finally, as to the significance of the tax for the banks. For the period 1901-1905, the tax on Massachusetts banks, exclusive of the amount paid on real estate, was equal to about nine per cent of their gross earnings, and to about twenty per cent of their net earnings.[1] For 1905 the tax on shares together with the tax on real estate amounts to over ten per cent of the gross income of the banks and to twenty-three per cent of their net income.[2] Regarded as a tax on the capital stock and surplus, the rate for 1905 was $16.54. While this rate is lower than the rate on corporate excess, it is about equal to the average tax on property in the state for 1905 ($16.83).

[1] The following table is based on data in the United States Comptroller's Report. The taxes there reported are the taxes on the shares, and do not include the value of real estate, so that the total taxes would be somewhat greater. The net earnings as used in the table include the taxes.

	Rate on capital and surplus.	Per cent of gross earnings.	Per cent of net earnings.
1901	$13.65	8.76	17.66
1902	13.96	9.86	21.09
1903	14.73	8.96	19.34
1904	14.13	8.90	18.04
1905	15.25	9.49	21.68

[2] For Massachusetts banking houses, furniture and fixtures the figures are given in the *Comptroller's report* for 1905 (p. 485) as $7,154,-933, on which the local taxes would be about $120,000.

Banks and trust companies present certain distinct features for taxation, which are due to the character of these corporations. In the first place, their assets are almost entirely intangible in character, whereas in the case of other corporations, tangible property is most important. In the second place, these corporations have no funded debt. The significance of these features for taxation may be briefly noted. The taxes paid by banks and trust companies are thus almost entirely taxes on intangible personal property. In this respect, that these corporations are taxed as fully on their intangible property as on tangible property, banks and trust companies are unique.[1] For in the case of other corporations, the existence of indebtedness in a large measure exempts intangible property and to no small degree even tangible property. In the case of business corporations, the law even makes provision for exempting intangible property beyond a certain maximum. And as for individuals, there is no effective method of reaching their intangible property. In the case of banks and trust companies, the corporation tax becomes therefore a very significant tax on intangible property.

Moreover, the fact that these corporations have no indebtedness means that the market value of the capital stock is a more adequate measure of the value of the corporation and its tax-paying ability for banks and trust companies than for other corporations. The practical consequence of this would therefore be to levy a heavier tax on banks and trust companies than on corporations generally.

On the other hand, banking institutions differ from busi-

[1] This is true to a less degree of trust companies, owing to the fact that they receive exemption for mortgages, an item which has little significance for banks. To a great extent this is also true of stock insurance companies, but these are allowed a deduction for property invested in bank shares.

ness corporations in a way which justifies a different treatment in taxation. The profits of a bank or trust company are due largely to operations carried on with the money of depositors, rather than to the investment of their original capital. Banks and trust companies are engaged in a branch of business carefully supervised by government, which affords thus a special opportunity for profit. The heavier tax may therefore be regarded as a payment for this special opportunity of gain.

III. *Taxation of Savings Banks.* Savings banks in Massachusetts are mutual, and are therefore taxed on the basis of their deposits. The tax has been imposed with a view to revenue for the state. The rate has, however, been made low, so as not to discourage deposits. Nevertheless, as the volume of deposits is large and grows constantly, the tax on savings banks has become, with the exception of the property tax, the largest single source of the state's income.

Previous to 1862 deposits in savings banks were taxable to the owner. But even with the aid of returns from the banks to the assessors, the percentage of deposits reached for taxation was small, not much over one-fifth of the total. The need for revenue, together with the inefficiency of taxation by the old method, led to the imposition of a tax on savings banks directly in 1862.[1] The rate was fixed at one-half of one per cent per annum on the deposits. The tax was made payable semi-annually, and levied on the average of the deposits for the six months preceding the date of assessment. The rate was then equivalent to one-half of the rate on general property. The tax was upheld as a tax on the franchise of savings banks.[2] After a number of changes, considerations of the revenue dictated an increase

---

[1] 1862, c. 224, § 4.   [2] 5 Allen, 428; 12 Allen, 312; 6 Wall., 611

of the rate in 1868 to three-fourths of one per cent,[1] and
this rate was continued until 1881, when the tax was fixed
at one-half of one per cent.[2]   This rate has remained unchanged.[3]

The nominal rate of taxation does not in itself indicate
the significance of the tax.   Previous to 1881 savings banks
either paid no tax on shares in national banks owned by
them, or received a refund of the tax on such shares.[4]   As
the amount thus invested was equivalent to ten per cent of
the deposits and the rate on bank shares was about double
the rate on deposits, this privilege meant in effect that
twenty per cent of their deposits were exempt from the
savings bank tax.   Furthermore savings banks were taxed on
their mortgages only through the tax on the deposits invested in loans on real estate.   Others lenders, however,
were taxable for these as for other property, or at double
the rate paid by the banks.   The sum invested in mortgages
during this period was equivalent to between forty and fifty
per cent of their total deposits.   In 1879 deposits invested in
real estate held by foreclosure were exempted.[5]   Thus
savings banks were exempted or favored in taxation for
more than half of their deposits throughout this earlier
period.

In 1881, when mortgages were relieved from taxation,
savings banks were freed by the same act from taxation on

[1] 1868, c. 315.   [2] 1881, c. 305, § 1.

[3] For an account of the changes in the state rate of tax on deposits,
and of the federal taxation of savings banks to 1872 see *Report of the
Tax Commission*, 1875, pp. 65-67.

[4] For data in regard to savings banks, and the taxes on their deposits see annual reports of the Commissioners of Savings Banks, and
the annual reports of the Treasurer to 1890 and thereafter the reports
of the Tax Commissioner.

[5] 1879, c. 115.

their investments in mortgages.[1] Deposits invested in real estate used for banking purposes were also made exempt.[2] As the rate of dividends paid by savings banks was declining, the rate of tax was at the same time reduced to one-half of one per cent.[3] In order, however, not to make too great inroads on the yield from the tax on savings banks the tax on their bank shares was no longer refunded to them;[4] only the amount invested in shares was exempted. The effect of these changes was to exempt about one-half of the deposits from taxation.[5] The rate, while nominally fixed at one-half of one per cent, became in reality one-fourth of one per cent, and the yield of the tax was reduced by more than one-half.

The savings bank tax was the subject of much controversy before 1881. It was criticized at the outset, because it deflected what had been local revenue to the state treasury, for the yield of the tax was retained by the state. Another contention was that, as the savings banks then paid from six to eight per cent in dividends, they were used by the wealthier classes for investment, in order to avoid the heavier property tax. The lower tax rate, it was urged, was unjustified, since it was not the savings of the masses that constituted the bulk of the deposits. On the other hand, it was argued that a great part of the deposits were

---

[1] 1881, c. 304, § 8.   [2] *Ibid.*, § 9.

[3] 1881, c. 305, § 1.

[4] See 1884, *House Doc.*, 380, p. 23; 1881, c. 305, § 2.

[5] Thus the average deposits for 1882 aggregated $252,988,000; the amount exempt because invested in bank stock, mortgages and real estate was $101,143,000. Of the total deposits for 1905—$662,808,000— the tax commissioner reports the amount taxable at $350,296,000. The date for the total deposits for 1905 as given by the savings banks commissioners is October thirty-first, whereas the date in the tax commissioner's report is May first.

owned in small sums, and would otherwise escape taxation, that many of the securities held by the banks were exempt, and that other property was taxed at a reduced valuation, so that on the whole the tax would about equal the tax on property.[1] In spite of much controversy the tax rate was not increased, and after 1875, as dividends began to decline, the plea was for reducing the rate. One other point to be noted with reference to this earlier period is that the changes in the rate of the tax do not seem to have exerted any influence on the amount of deposits.

From the point of view of the revenue of the state, the savings bank tax has always constituted a very large item, rising from more than ten per cent for 1861-1870 to nearly thirty per cent for 1871-1875 and almost forty per cent for the next five years. The exemption of mortgages from taxation and the reduction of the rate of the tax in 1881 led to the loss of more than one-half of the tax on savings banks. From $1,613,606, in 1881,[2] the revenue fell to $923,906 in 1882, and $757,720 in 1883. It then gradually rose again until, for 1905, the tax amounted to $1,751,481, a sum greater than the income of the state from the general corporation tax and the bank tax. For the period since 1880, from seventeen and a half to twenty per cent of the total state revenue has come from the savings bank tax.

From these historical considerations we turn to the present situation. Savings banks are taxed at the rate of one-half of one per cent on the average of their deposits. The amount of deposits exempted, however, constitutes nearly fifty per cent of their total deposits and more than fifty per cent of their total funds, so that the tax is in effect about

[1] For this controversy, see *Report of Tax Commission* of 1875, pp. 60-66 and 427-430. In addition to the references there given, see 1863 *House Document* 184; 1869 *House Document* 329.

[2] See *Auditor's Report* for 1881, p. 13.

one-fourth of one per cent.[1]   This is the real significance of
the tax to the depositor, who is interested in the relation of
the tax to the total deposits and to the amount that would
otherwise be available for dividends.[2]   From the point of
view of earnings, the tax paid on deposits for 1901-1905
amounts to five and one-half per cent of the gross earnings
of savings banks, and is equal to six and one-half per cent of
the total amount that might otherwise go to dividends.
The tax on savings banks can not be said to operate
with perfect equality on the different banks.   The reason
is that the tax, levied on the amount of deposits,[3] can not
take account of the net earnings.[4]

[1] Deposits have been defined by court decision to be the amount due
and payable to depositors, the amount deposited by them together
with all interest and dividends accruing and payable thereon. (151
Mass., 103.) There are thus exempt from taxation: (1) the guarantee
fund and undivided earnings; and likewise deposits invested in (2)
real estate used for banking purposes, in (3) real estate held by foreclosure, and (4) in mortgage loans ($286,385,000). Savings banks
receive, moreover, a refund of the tax on so much of their deposits
as is invested in (5) bank shares. For 1905 the total amount held
by savings banks is reported as $707,728,000, the deposits amounted to
$662,808,000, the amount exempted was $355,117,000.

[2] For the years 1901-1905 the tax actually paid on deposits, deducting the amount returned from the bank tax, equals, on the average,
0.23 per cent of all the funds held by the savings banks, or 0.24 per
cent of their deposits. Including the amount paid for taxes on real
estate (assuming the same rate as for corporate excess) the total
taxes for 1905 would equal 0.26 per cent of the total assets and 0.28
per cent of their deposits.

[3] Thus for 1905, 92 banks paid 3½ per cent and 82 banks paid 4 per
cent in dividends. The latter would naturally pay a smaller tax on
their net earnings than the former.

[4] The Massachusetts Hospital Life Insurance Company pays on
money and property held by it in trust, for deposit or investment, at
the same rate as the savings banks (1862, c. 224, § 3; 1865, c. 283,
§ 18). The amount of tax paid in 1905 was $58,203. There was also
for a time a tax on co-operative banks (1877, c. 224, § 18; 1878, c.
250), but the revenue derived from this source was insignificant, and
the tax was abolished in 1890 (c. 63).

The rate of the tax on deposits seems very low when viewed as a tax on property. However, disregarding the questions relating to ownership of the deposits, and the desirability of encouraging savings, two considerations are to be borne in mind. In the first place, the deposits are invested almost exclusively in intangible property, and intangible personalty in general escapes even in Massachusetts. In proof of this fact we need only point out that the personal estate reached by the assessors exclusive of the bank stock which can not escape, amounted, in 1905, to only $679,769,000.[1] In this connection we recall that the tax commission of 1897[2] found that probably more than one-half of the personalty taxed was tangible in character. This would mean that only about $300,000,000 of intangible property, comparable with savings bank investments, are reached. Against this comparatively small sum, the deposits of savings banks amounted for the same year to $662,808,000 and their total assets to $707,728,000.[3] The tax on savings banks thus reaches property of a character that in general escapes taxation.

The second consideration is that the law, in the interest of safety, restricts investments to securities bearing a low rate of interest. Thus of the assets amounting to $707,-728,000, mortgages alone constitute forty per cent, and public funds, railroad and street railway bonds, and deposits on interest in banks aggregate over thirty per cent. From the point of view of income the rate of the tax is in itself not very low and, at the same time, not excessive.

Remembering, however, that property of the kind as-

[1] *Aggregates of Polls, Property and Taxes* for 1905, p. 59.

[2] *Report of the Tax Commission*, 1897, particularly p. 49.

[3] For data see *Report of the Savings Bank Commissioners* for 1905, p. 745.

sessed to the savings banks in general escapes, the savings bank tax can scarcely be justified as a tax on property or income, in view of the actual inefficiency of the methods of taxing intangible personalty. On the other hand, the savings banks of Massachusetts are mutual, and the supervision of the state provides the depositor with a cheap and safe agency for investment.[1] The tax may be regarded rather as a charge on the depositor for this service by the government. The practical reason for the tax is, however, that institutions for savings afford a ready and certain source of revenue to the state.

IV. *Insurance Companies—Fire and Marine.*—The taxation of the business of fire and marine insurance may be dated from the Civil War. Previous to 1862, Massachusetts stock insurance companies were taxed on their shares like other corporations, and mutual companies were exempt. Insurance companies from other states were taxed, except for a few years, only under retaliatory taxes. Companies from foreign countries were not given special attention for taxation until 1856. The policy of Massachusetts had thus been to refrain from taxing the business of insurance for the purpose of revenue.

In 1862 there came a charge of policy. Owing to the need of revenue a tax was imposed on all fire and marine insurance companies. Massachusetts joint-stock insurance companies were a little later treated like other corporations having a capital stock and brought under the general corporation tax. Other companies, however, both foreign and domestic, were reached through a tax on their premiums; in other words, a tax on gross receipts. A desire to foster home industry dictated, however, a lower rate for domestic corporations than for foreign insurance companies.

[1] See in this connection the *Report of the Tax Commission*, 1897, p. 72.

A. Massachusetts stock insurance companies are, at present, with one exception, engaged in fire and marine insurance. In 1862 they were taxed, like other domestic insurance companies, at one per cent on their premiums.[1] This tax was in addition to the tax on their corporate shares. In 1864 stock insurance companies were brought under the general corporation tax law.[2] These corporations were, however, granted a return of the tax on bank shares held by them, in order to reduce their tax burden.[3] When in 1880 the law made provision for taxing life insurance companies on their premiums, no exception was made for stock insurance companies, with the consequence that the Massachusetts stock life insurance company pays a tax on both its capital and its premiums. In 1884 title guarantee companies were made taxable like stock insurance companies.[4]

Massachusetts stock companies have not proved successful in insurance, and the tax derived from this class of corporations has been declining, as may be seen from the diminishing amounts paid on their corporate excess. In 1871 they paid $176,526. After the Boston fire the amount dropped to $106,226 in 1875. In 1880 the sum was $140,710. By 1890 it had declined to $86,212, and in 1905 to $65,217.

Even after deducting the tax on bank shares (amounting to $19,378 in 1905) these companies pay at a much greater

---

[1] 1862, c. 224, § 1. This tax on premiums was not removed until 1872 (c. 245).

[2] See 1864, c. 208, § 7. See also 1865, c. 283, § 18.

[3] The guarantee capital or permanent fund of mutual fire and marine insurance companies was at the recommendation of the tax commissioner made taxable like the capital stock of insurance companies. See 98 Mass., 25, *Tax Commissioner's Report* for 1869, p. 14; 1872, c. 375, § 12.

[4] 1884, c. 180, § 5; 1887, c. 214, § 64.

rate on their business than foreign companies.[1]   They pro-
tested against their tax in 1882,[2] and in 1887 the insurance
commissioner urged that their taxes be reduced, in order
to keep the capital still engaged in the business of insurance
from leaving it.   Again in 1890, Governor Brackett suggested [3] that they be taxed on their premiums, pointing out
that they paid twice the amount they would pay as foreign
corporations.[4]   But no exception was made in their case
from the general law taxing corporations on their capital
stock, and the discrimination against these companies in
favor of their foreign rivals continues.

B. In the taxation of insurance companies other than
those engaged in life insurance, Massachusetts favors her
mutual companies by taxing them at one-half the rate imposed on foreign companies.   In 1862 [5] an annual tax of one
per cent on all premiums and assessments received by them

---

[1] Report of the Insurance Commissioner for 1887, pp. xv-xvii.
Here it is shown that the Massachusetts stock insurance companies
paid for 1886, $77,970, where as foreign companies paying a tax of
two per cent on their premiums, their taxes would have been $38,824
(p. xv).

[2] 1882 Sen. Doc., 279; 1883 Sen. Doc., 1, p. 4.

[3] 1890 Sen. Doc., 1, pp. 27-29.

[4] In 1905 Massachusetts fire and marine companies received in
premiums $1,001,175 for Massachusetts business. The tax for the
four fire and marine insurance companies amounts to $61,283. The
entire amount refunded on the bank tax to all stock insurance companies was $19,378, Massachusetts fire and stock insurance com-
panies are thus paying more than twice as much on their business as
they would pay if taxed like foreign companies, that is, two per cent
on their premiums. This is manifestly unjust. There is but one
stock life insurance company in Massachusetts. Its taxes in 1905
were $1,802, a sum from which it would be free as a foreign com-
pany. The total tax on stock insurance companies amounted in 1905
to $65,217. Deducting the amount refunded on their bank shares, the
tax is $45,839.

[5] 1862, c. 224, § 1; 1865, c. 283, § 18; 1868, c. 165; 1873, c. 141.

was imposed, payable in semi-annual instalment.[1]   In 1865 the law was modified so as to exempt them from the payment of the tax on premiums received in other states, where they are subject to a like tax.

Insurance companies incorporated in other states are taxed at the rate of two per cent on their premiums received in Massachusetts.[2]   While they pay at a rate equal to double the rate on domestic mutual companies, they are favored in turn as against companies from foreign countries.   In 1878 associations on the plan of the Lloyds, whether of Massachusetts citizens or of citizens of other states, were made subject to taxation at the same rate.[3]   This two per cent rate has been applied to all forms of insurance except life insurance carried on by companies having a charter from another state.[4]   Massachusetts, moreover, still retains her reciprocal tax provision and foreign companies from states where Massachusetts companies are taxed at a higher rate are subject to a tax equal to the highest rate imposed on Massachusetts corporations.[5]

Insurance companies from foreign countries were for a long time taxed at a rate that would be protective to both Massachusetts and domestic corporations.   One reason urged for such a discrimination against alien companies was that Massachusetts companies did not carry on business abroad as they did in the other American states.   In 1862 the tax imposed was four per cent of the premiums received in

---

[1] Only the premiums retained by the companies are taxable, deduction being allowed for return premiums and sums paid for re-insurance. This applies to all companies taxed on their premiums.

[2] 1862, c. 224, § 2; 1873, c. 141, § 2.

[3] 1878, c. 218, § 3.

[4] 1887, c. 214.

[5] R. L., 118, § 85.

Massachusetts.[1]   After the Boston fire a more lenient policy was adopted.[2]   Insurance companies from foreign countries, which keep on deposit, with the proper authorities of one of the states, approved investments to the amount of two hundred thousand dollars for the security of American policy holders, were treated like American companies from other states and taxed at the rate of two per cent on their premiums.   At the present time only companies which do not comply with this requirement pay the four per cent tax.[3]

Companies engaged in branches of insurance outside of life insurance are thus variously taxed; domestic stock companies on their capital, domestic mutual companies at one per cent of their premiums; foreign American companies, and companies from abroad complying with certain requirements, at two per cent, and other alien companies at four per cent. There does not seem to be any guiding principle here, other than protection to Massachusetts mutual companies.

[1] 1862, c. 224, § 2.

[2] 1873, c. 141, § 4. See also 1872, chs. 228, 325. This policy was not satisfactory to Massachusetts stock companies, which sought to have a four per cent tax imposed on all alien companies. The measure proposed was, however, not adopted, it being shown that the advantage to the community in a lower premium far outbalanced the gain that might come from a higher rate of tax. See 1882 *Sen. Doc.*, 279 (particularly the minority report); also J. H. Benton, *Argument against Bill to increase the Tax upon Foreign Insurance Companies*, etc., Boston, 1882, and a similar pamphlet by Geo. O. Shattuck of the same date.

[3] In addition to the tax on foreign companies there is imposed an annual license fee of two dollars on their agents. There is also an annual license fee of ten dollars levied on insurance brokers (R. L., c. 118, §§ 88, 90). The net income from licenses amounted in 1905 to $66,480. A special license fee of twenty dollars annually is imposed on the privilege of insuring, under certain conditions, with companies not authorized to do business in the state. Such companies are then taxed at four per cent on the amount of their premiums (1887, c. 214). The income from this source is small, amounting in 1905 to $3,265.

The revenue from insurance companies, other than Massachusetts stock companies, is large and has been growing steadily. Thus for 1876-1880 these taxes average $125,-762, for 1886-90 $189,578. For 1896-1900 the figures are $289,349, and, for 1901-1905, $405,801. The amount paid in 1905 was $446,059. To this sum mutual companies contributed probably less than $50,000.[1] Adding to these taxes for 1905 the amounts received from insurance licenses ($69,745) and the net tax received from Massachusetts stock companies (about $40,000) the total revenue aggregated about $550,000. Of this total more than four-fifths is paid by foreign insurance compaines.

The discrimination in the rate of tax on insurance companies is evidently not the determining factor in their competition for insurance business in Massachusetts. The advantage of one per cent in taxation has not sufficed to give Massachusetts mutual companies a preponderant part of the business in the state. On the contrary, the portion of the business done by Massachusetts companies, which are chiefly mutual, has been declining.[2]

V. *Life Insurance Companies.*—Life insurance was for a long time regarded as a form of industry to be encouraged rather than taxed and was therefore left exempt even after

---

[1] The premiums reported for mutual companies in 1905 amount to $4,747,000.

[2] The proportion of the total risks written in Massachusetts by companies is as follows:

	1886.	1890.	1900.	1905.
Massachusetts	36	31	24	19
Other American	40	42	41	44
Alien.	22	26	34	35

The proportion of the total risks written by the Massachusetts joint stock companies has declined from 15 per cent in 1886 to 4 per cent in 1905. For data see the annual reports of the Insurance Commissioner.

other branches of insurance had been made a source of revenue to the state. " The business of mutual life insurance has never been treated by the legislature as an appropriate object of taxation. A tax upon it is, in effect, a tax on prudence," [1] is a view expressed in a court decision. Not therefore until 1880 was a tax imposed. [2] The rate was first established at one-half of one per cent, and then at one-quarter of one per cent, of the net value of all policies in force within the state. [3] No distinction was made between domestic and foreign companies.

The theory of the legislature in imposing this tax was that life insurance companies should be treated for taxation like savings banks. Both were investing the savings of the citizens. As summed up by the court, in its decision upholding the tax, the object of the legislature was to impose an excise upon such associations as by virtue of their franchise exercise the function of receiving from many citizens money as trustees to invest and to manage for them. [4] Cooperative associations and insurance companies conducting their business so as not to create net values, are exempt.

The basis of the tax is the sum which, with interest and future payments, will provide for the payment of the policy. This is a deviation from the usual method of taxing insurance companies on their premiums. The rate, one-fourth of one per cent, is, as we have seen, substantially the rate on

[1] 98 Mass., 28.

[2] For earlier proposals to tax life insurance see *Report of the Tax Commission*, 1875, pp. 175-176, and Appendix, 459-468. See also *Auditor's Report* for 1869, p. 15, and 1870 *House Doc.*, 248, p. 7.

[3] 1880, c. 227, § 1 ; 1881, c. 219.

[4] 133 Mass., 161 ; see also the fuller exposition in the *Report of the Tax Commissioner* for 1880, pp. 12-16. For criticism see *Report of the Insurance Commissioner* for 1879, pt. ii, pp. xv-xviii, and for 1880, pt. ii, p. xxiii.

savings banks. In effect, however, the tax is heavier, amounting to a little more than one per cent of the premiums.[1] At this rate Massachusetts taxes life insurance companies more leniently than most states, two per cent on the gross premiums [2] being the usual percentage exacted in the form of a tax.[3]

[1] For data see reports of premiums received in Massachusetts as given by the Insurance Commissioner, and the taxes as reported by the auditor.

[2] See summary of the insurance taxes in the various states, in the *Report of the California Commission on Revenue and Taxation,* 1906, pp. 260.

[3] There is also retained a retaliatory clause in the law, whereby insurance companies of states discriminating in taxation against Massachusetts companies are taxed at the highest rate imposed on Massachusetts companies. A small fee to defray the expense of valuing the policies of life insurance companies is also imposed on the companies. *R. I.,* c. 118, §§ 33, 11, 75, 76. The income from this source in 1905 was $16,986. The tax on life insurance companies yielded in 1881, when it was first assessed at its present rate, $96,743. The income has increased steadily, amounting to $120,434 in 1890; $219,395 in 1900, and $306,974 in 1905, or more than three times the amount in 1881.

CHAPTER VII

Summary and Conclusion

Turning from the details of the taxation of corporations in Massachusetts, we shall endeavor, at this point, to bring together the threads of historical development, to indicate the influences shaping the corporation taxes, to summarize the essential features in the existing system, and to point out the importance for the taxation of corporations of the relation of government to corporate activity.

1. *Historical Development.*—With the industrial development of Massachusetts, following the Revolution came corporate activity. The adoption of corporate organization in business brought with it the problem of taxing corporations. As at the close of the eighteenth century the general property tax had become well nigh the exclusive form of taxation in the state, this general tax was applied to the new form of wealth, consisting in corporate shares. The intent of the general property tax being to assess all wealth on the basis of its market value, the same rule was applied to corporate stock, and it was taxed together with other personal estate to the owner.

Originally not only the shareholders were taxed but the corporation as such was also taxed for its property. This double taxation was then partially obviated by freeing the corporations from taxation on their personal property. For manufacturing companies, moreover, the law in 1832 made provision for taxing all their property, and at the same time for avoiding double taxation.   Real estate and machinery was made taxable to the corporation in the place where it was situated, for the local authorities could best assess this form of property.   The value of the shares, after deducting a proportionate amount for the property taxed directly to the corporation, was assessed to the individual owners of the shares.   This method of taxing property in corporations, on the basis of the market value of the shares, was applicable, however, only to corporations having a capital stock, divided into shares, that is, corporations engaged in business for private profit.   All such corporations were taxed essentially alike.

Financial corporations were treated differently for taxation.   With reference to mutual corporations, like insurance companies and savings banks, the policy of the state was to encourage their activity, and they were accordingly left exempt from direct taxation.   Banks, on the other hand, were subjected to a special tax, in addition to the general property tax levied on their shares.   Banks were dependent in the earlier period on special charters, so that the bank charter conferred a valuable privilege.   The special impost on these institutions was regarded as a payment for the special favor conferred by the state.

The Civil War wrought a great change in the system of taxing corporations.   The growing need for revenue to meet expenditures occasioned by the war, led the state to abandon its policy of exemption to savings banks and insurance companies, and to reform its method of taxing the other corporations so as to reach more fully their intangible property.   With a view to creating sources of revenues for the state independent of the property tax, taxes were levied on fire and marine insurance, and on deposits in savings banks.   Two decades later an excise was imposed also on life insurance.   In the absence of a capital stock, the tax on fire and marine insurance companies was levied on the basis of premiums; for savings banks, the average deposits were made the measure for the impost; and for life insurance companies, the tax was assessed on the net value of the policies. The rate of the charge was made low in the case of these corporations, so as not to discourage their activity. Nevertheless they afforded the state a large and ever-increasing revenue.

For corporations having a capital stock, and organized for private gain, the tax on shares was found to be an inefficient means of reaching fully the property of corporations. The increasing burden of taxation prompted the establishment of a more effective machinery for this purpose. A centralized state agency was substituted for the local assessor, in the administration of the tax. Instead of assessing the shareholder, the state turned to the corporation, and stopped the tax at the source. Corporations organized for private profit, having a capital stock divided into shares were made taxable on the market value of their capital stock. Real estate and machinery were left for assessment by the local assessors. To avoid double taxation, the state commissioner, therefore, deducts the value of the property taxed by local authorities from the value of the capital stock, levying the state tax only on the remainder, or corporate excess. Corporate debts were regarded in the same light as debts owed by individuals, and remained taxable to the creditor, that is the bondholder. The basis of the tax on corporations, their capital stock alone, does not, therefore, represent the entire value of the corporation.

The practices of the property tax were continued in the rate imposed on corporations and in the distribution of the proceeds, the purpose being to tax the corporations in the same way as the individuals had been taxed for their shares. The rate was made a close approximation to the average rate on general property.   The proceeds are distributed to the cities and towns in which the shareholders reside.   Only so much as would be due on the shares of non-residents of the state is assigned to the state treasury.   The national banks, which had replaced the earlier state banks, could not be included in this general corporation tax, on account of their federal charters.   The method adopted for taxing them is however substantially the same: they too are taxed on their capital stock.

All domestic corporations organized for profit were thus made taxable in essentially the same way.   The most important classes of foreign corporations, those engaged in public-service enterprises, were also included under the law. Foreign manufacturing and mercantile corporations not having assumed great importance until more recently were left to the general property tax.   Massachusetts thus developed one general method for taxing all her corporations that are engaged in business primarily for private gain. This was achieved by levying a tax on all of them alike on the basis of the market value of their capital stock.

The closing decade of the nineteenth century brought with it a more complex corporate activity, which was reflected also in the law taxing corporations.   With the varied application of electricity to the field of public-service enterprises, municipal utility corporations assumed a new importance.   The municipalities demanded a compensation for the special franchise granted by them, and also that the tax on the corporate excess of these companies should be allotted to the cities and towns from which these corporations derived their earnings.   In the case of the most important of this class of corporations, the street railways, the legislature complied with this demand.   It assigned the tax collected by the state to the municipalities served.   At the same time it made provision for a division of profits with the public, when dividends should exceed eight per cent. No revenue has, however, been derived from this tax. For the other municipal utility corporations, no change in the law has as yet been effected.

The close of the nineteenth century saw also a rapid adoption of the corporate form of organization for ordinary business. At the same time it became increasingly frequent for corporations to conduct business in Massachusetts under foreign charter. Since the general corporation tax did not apply to these foreign companies there was no way of reaching their corporate excess. Under the general property tax they would in many instances be subject to a smaller burden than the domestic corporations. This applied to corporations whose assets consisted largely of intangible property, or whose shares exceeded the value of their tangible property. To remove this incentive to adopt foreign charters, the tax on the corporate excess on business corporations was reduced, so that manufacturing and mercantile corporations are taxable, at the maximum, on little more than their tangible property. At the same time a slight excise was imposed on foreign corporations. The attempt to tax business corporations on intangible property has thus met with little more success than the similar endeavor to reach the intangible property of individuals.

The general corporation tax, in its original form, therefore, applies now only to public-service corporations and financial corporations. These are still taxed on the entire value of their capital stock. The motive here is, obviously, to reach elements, other than tangible property, that enter into the value of the capital stock. Another reason for taxing the full value of the capital stock of public-service corporations, is to be found in the fact that much of their tangible property is exempt from local assessment. It is to be noted that the two classes of corporations taxed on the basis of their capital stock are made up of corporations which are subject to government regulation and control. The general corporation tax has thus, in the main, become a tax on special branches of corporate business, which are the recipients of government favor, or which are subject to government regulation.

2. *Influences in the Development of the Corporation Taxes.*—In the development of the Massachusetts system of taxing corporations, we may observe three influences at work in determining the burden to be imposed on corporate activity. The most important factor has been the general property tax. This is still at the basis of the system of taxing all corporations organized for the purposes of private gain. The excise levied on the capital stock was intended to supplement the tax on the tangible property of corporations, and to reach elements which give value to a corporation, but which elude the local assessors. The second motive has been the desire to exact compensation for a special privilege conferred by the state. This motive dictated the tax levied on the state banks up to the close of the Civil War. More recently it has led to the adoption of a provision for a special franchise tax on street railways. This too is the implied justification for taxing public service corporations by a method under which more than their tangible property may be reached; for intangible property in the hand of individuals and business corporations has very largely become exempt. A third element in determining the tax burden to be imposed has been the desire to encourage certain forms of corporate activity the social benefit of which is widespread. For this reason mutual insurance companies were left exempt before the war, and no tax was imposed directly on savings banks. Later, when the state resorted to a tax on them for revenue, the rate imposed was made low, so as not to discourage their activity.

The relation of government to corporate activity has thus expressed itself in three policies in the taxation of corporations: taxation under the general property tax, or an approximation to it, where corporations, organized for purposes of private gain, receive no special favor from government, or require no particular regulation; special taxation, where the corporate activity is dependent on special privilege or requires government regulation; and leniency or exemption from taxation where the corporations may be regarded as acting in the capacity of trustees, and private gain is not the chief object of their activity. These principles of taxation are present in the tax system rather as tendencies; their practical application is yet far from completely realized.

Administrative motives have likewise played a part in shaping the corporation taxes. The change from the taxation of persons to the taxation of corporations was due to the difficulties experienced in attempting to reach corporate shares and savings bank deposits in the hands of the individual owners. The significant point, here, is, however, that the assessment of corporations instead of individuals involved a further deviation from the principle of individual ability or faculty as the basis of the tax. A tax on the corporation is not the same as a tax on the stockholder. The tax is regarded by the corporation as an item of expense. Its shares, at a time when intangible personal property in general escapes, will have a market value determined by the net earnings, after the tax on the corporation has been deducted. The purchaser of the stock thus escapes the tax. In the case of corporations, as earlier in the case of real estate, and again in the case of tangible personal property, administrative considerations led to the ignoring of persons in taxation.

Another administrative motive in the development of the

corporation taxes, has been the desire to provide for the state sources of revenue independent of the general property tax. The imposition of the bank tax before the war was due to this cause, and the revenue from this source long enabled the state to dispense with the state levy on property. The present taxes on savings banks and insurance companies have been made sources of state revenue with the same end in view. The segregation of source has not however been carried, in Massachusetts, to a point which would assign all the corporation taxes to the state, or which would render the state independent of the tax on general property.

3. *Present Significance of the Corporation Taxes.*—Two groups of corporations are to be distinguished with reference to taxation, according as the primary object of their activity is private gain or not. The first group is by far the most important from both the economic and fiscal point of view. It is made up of the various public-service corporations, financial corporations, such as banks, trust companies and stock insurance companies, and business corporations, that is, mercantile and manufacturing companies. These corporations contribute about two-thirds of the yield of the imposts on corporations. Disregarding differences in detail, the common element in the method of taxing all these companies is that the basis of the tax is the capital stock. State and local authorities co-operate in assessing the taxes on these corporations. The local authorities levy the general property tax on their real estate and machinery, the state commissioner assesses the tax on the corporate excess. State and municipality likewise share in the revenue derived from the tax on corporate excess. The greater part of the yield is apportioned among the cities and towns according to the residence of the shareholders. The state retains so much of the tax as corresponds to the shares owned by non-residents of the state.

Although all these corporations are taxed alike on the basis of their capital stock, the tax has a different meaning for the various classes of corporations. Manufacturing corporations pay by far the greater part of their total taxes locally on their real estate and machinery. The corporate excess represents very largely tangible property that is exempt from local taxation. For mercantile corporations the same is true. With the limitation set by the law to the corporate excess on which business corporations are liable to taxation, the maximum on which a corporation can be assessed is little more than the value of its tangible property. With the privilege allowed to corporations to offset their merchandise and other tangible personalty by debts, business corporations, taking the group as a whole, are taxed on much less than their tangible property. Moreover as very often there are no quotations available for the stock of such corporations, property becomes very largely the measure of the tax, and not capitalized earnings.

For public-service corporations the tax on corporate excess becomes a very important supplement to the property tax. This is due in a large measure to the fact that the tangible personalty of such corporations is to a great extent exempt from local assessment, and this is true also of part of the real estate of railroads. Hence public service corporations pay more on their corporate excess than they pay on their property taxed by the local assessors. In some instances the total taxes paid are more than would be due if merely tangible property were assessed. Here, too, the tax on corporations is based, to a very great extent, on the market value of the stocks, so that the tax is levied on capitalized earnings. However, as bonds are not included in the taxable valuation of the corporation, and the bondholder generally escapes local assessment, the tax is levied on only part of the capitalized earnings.

Financial institutions, like banks and trust companies, are assessed to a greater degree than the corporations considered above, on their capitalized earnings. As these corporations have little tangible property, they pay but a small part of their taxes to the local authorities. The corporate excess, therefore, represents intangible property. Moreover, as banks and trust companies have no bonded indebtedness the value of their capital stock is more nearly the capitalization of total net earnings than in the case of other corporations. These institutions would, therefore, be apt to be taxed more fully than other corporations.

Of the total taxes levied by the state on all corporations, about two-thirds comes from these three classes. About one-third of the total corporation taxes is derived from the public-service group, the railroads, and the municipal utility companies furnishing nearly equal amounts. The financial group comes second in importance from the fiscal point of view, yielding more than a half of the amount paid by the public-service corporations. Mercantile and manufacturing companies contribute somewhat less.

It becomes evident, both from the significance of the corporate excess for the various classes of corporations and from the amount of revenue yielded by them, that the real problem in the taxation of corporations organized for private profit is the taxation of public-service and financial corporations. For the taxation of business corporations, the method employed under the general corporation tax has an administrative superiority over the necessarily more lax methods of the general property tax; it does not however reach more than property. For public-service corporations the tax on corporate excess reaches tangible property that can not be dealt with at all adequately by local assessors, and to an extent it reaches more than property. For financial corporations, the tax on corporate excess is more than a property tax.

The most important criticism on the present method of taxing these corporations pertains to the basis of the tax. This is the market value of the capital stock alone.[1] The advantage of this method lies in its simplicity. It avoids the necessity of any elaborate assessment by a state board. Moreover stocks represent a proportion of the property of Massachusetts corporations that is far larger than the proportion represented by bonds. Furthermore the strict control, exercised by Massachusetts over the issue of securities, makes the market value of stocks less objectionable a basis, because they are less subject to manipulation for speculative purposes.

The chief objection, however, is that a tax on the market value of stocks alone, when there are bonds outstanding, is necessarily an inadequate measure both of the net earnings and of the property of a corporation. Bonds were originally excluded in determining the taxable value of the corporation, on the theory that bonds are a debt, rather than a preferred interest in the corporation. They are by law taxable under the general property tax, but such property is very seldom discovered by the assessor. In consequence of this inadequate basis for the taxation of corporations, there results inequality both as between different corporations and as between different groups of corporations. Those that are heavily bonded bear a lighter burden than

---

[1] For the detailed criticism of capital stock as a basis for taxing corporations, see Seligman, *Essays in Taxation*, pp. 193-4, and Adams, *Science of Finance*, p. 456. The criticisms apply with some modifications, in view of Massachusetts conditions. See also the criticisms, from the point of view of the taxation of railroads, made by California Commission on Revenue and Taxation in its report, p. 116, and the Ontario Commission on Railway Taxation (*Report*, p. 117).

those whose property is represented to a greater degree or wholly by stocks. The basis of the tax therefore results not only in inadequate taxation, but also in unequal taxation.[1]

In harmony with the present method of taxing corporations on the basis of the market value of their securities, the natural reform would be to levy the tax on the aggregate market value of both stocks and bonds, as has recently been proposed for public-service corporations by a legislative committee. Theoretically even this basis for a tax is not free from objection,[2] as compared with a direct tax on net earnings. A tax based on the value of both stocks and bonds, under Massachusetts conditions, would, however, be a close approximation to the more ideal tax based on net earnings.

A tax on this basis of stocks and bonds would not be free from other objections. In the first place, this would involve the adoption of a method of taxation for these corporations totally different from the method employed in assessing individuals and business corporations. These latter are taxed, in the main, on property and rather leniently on tangible personal property. Unless a rate lower than the property rate were adopted, the effect would obviously be to impose a higher tax on public-service and financial corporations than on other tax payers. Equality would thus be established as between these corporations, but not as between these cor-

---

[1] This criticism applies particularly to the tax as it operates on public-service corporations. A similar criticism is to be directed to the tax on business corporations. Here the basis of the tax is either the capital stock or the net assets. In either case corporations with a larger indebtedness escape with a lighter tax. Moreover, the creation of indebtedness can be used as a means of evading taxation, sometimes completely.

[2] For criticisms, see Seligman, *op. cit.*, pp. 195, 211-212, 262; Adams, *op. cit.*, 456-7.

porations and other tax payers. This method of taxation would, therefore, mean the special taxation of corporations.

Another criticism of a tax based on both stocks and bonds is that it would levy a tax on all corporations alike, whether their franchise conferred a special monopoly advantage or not. It would thus still be necessary to supplement such a tax by a special franchise tax, where the franchise confers extraordinary earning power, as the law at present attempts to do in the case of street railways.

The Massachusetts system of taxing corporations organized for private profit is thus unsatisfactory from the point of view of both theory and practice. On the other hand the method employed has been efficient in yielding a large and increasing revenue. Hence, there has been comparativly little complaint. The efficiency of the system is, however, due in part to Massachusetts conditions, already noted.[1] It would therefore not be equally efficient under other conditions,[2] and, in its present form, it can not be regarded as a model for other states.

The other group of corporations made up of savings banks and life insurance companies has yielded the state a large and growing revenue. These taxes, and particularly the tax on savings banks, reach a large amount of intangible wealth, which ordinarily escapes taxation in the hands of individuals. The tax is at a low rate, and there is no complaint. In view of the actual enforcement of the tax on intangible personal property, it would appear that these corporations are taxed for property which generally escapes taxation. The control by the state over these corporations thus enables it to derive a revenue from property which can not be successfully taxed to individuals.

[1] *Vide supra*, p. 173.

[2] See the references already cited to the Reports of the Ontario and California Commissions.

4. *Corporation Taxes and the Relation of the Government to Corporations.*—In conclusion we wish to note the importance which the relation of the state to corporations has for the taxation of corporations. In the first place the state requires from the corporations sworn returns. This means that the corporation taxes rest on a more accurate basis than the assessor's guess. This also differentiates corporations from individuals for taxation, for in the case of individuals returns to the assessor have well-nigh ceased. In consequence it becomes impossible to tax individuals for income or for intangible property; and even the taxation of tangible personal property must rest on the assessor's estimate. Returns of corporations, on the other hand, render it possible to tax corporations on intangible property or on earnings, and thus furnish a better basis for taxation.

More important, however, is the fact, that corporation taxes, so far as they have more than an administrative significance, have become taxes on branches of business to which the government stands in a peculiarly intimate relation. Outside of the business corporations, where the corporate excess stands for little more than the property exempt to corporations from local assessment, the taxes are paid by public-service corporations, and by the financial institutions, that is, banks, trust companies, savings banks, and insurance companies. All of these corporations are subject to government supervision and regulation.

Public-service corporations, which as we have seen yield so large a part of the revenue, and of these more particularly the municipal utility corporations, are most closely dependent on government. They receive from the community a franchise conferring a monopoly privilege, and in turn are subject to regulation by the state. As such regulation seeks, on the one hand, to protect the public from exorbitant charges, and, on the other, to secure to the corporation a reasonable profit, the question of the taxation of public-service corporations must be closely connected with the problem of their control.[1] Taxes form an item of expenditure that must be deducted before dividends can be paid. If we disregard the practical considerations, which may however be most important, the tax would thus become an element in the cost of the service to the public, and therefore an indirect burden imposed on the public. Until recently public-service corporations have been taxed like other corporations. The trend at present seem to be in favor of utilizing municipal utility corporations as a special source of revenue rather than to attempt the more difficult task of reducing the cost of the service to the consumer.

In the taxation of the financial corporations, it is again branches of business under government supervision on which the tribute is levied. In the case of banks and trust companies, the method employed results in taxing these corporations to a greater degree than other corporate enterprise. In the case of savings banks and insurance companies, the government is enabled by its control of these institutions to exact a tax on property which generally escapes assessment to individuals. The taxation of corporations is thus intimately bound up with government regulation and control of corporations.

[1] See also W. Z. Ripley in *Publications of the American Economic Association*, series 3, vol. 2, pp. 117 *et seq.*

APPENDIX

TAXES ON STREET RAILWAYS.

AVERAGES FOR 1903-1905. (In thousands of dollars.)

| | Per Cent of Earnings from Operation. All Taxes. | | Local and Corporate Excess. | | Per Cent of Interest to Total Amount Paid on Bonds and Stocks. | Average Amount of Taxes on Property and Corporate Excess. | Hypothetical Taxes on Earnings from Operation. | | Ratio of Operating Expenses to Earnings from Operation. |
| | Gross. | Net. | Gross. | Net. | | | Gross. 5% per cent. | Net. 17½ per cent. | |
	I.	II.	III.	IV.	V.	VI.	VII.	VIII.	IX.
Boston Elevated	7.8	25.0	6.9	22.2	26	$85	$679	$672	68.5
Boston and Northern	5.6	17.1	3.5	10.5	66	133	209	221	66.5
Boston and Worcester	6.8	14.5	4.9	10.4	46	20	23	34	51.8
Holyoke	7.1	23.0	4.9	15.9	34	18	20	20	68.9
Old Colony	5.9	18.8	4.0	12.8	61	96	130	131	68.2
Springfield	7.7	27.9	5.5	19.9	25	53	52	46	72.0
Union	9.1	25.4	7.0	19.6	20	25	20	23	64.0
Worcester Consolidated	7.9	20.1	5.7	14.5	20	77	74	93	60.1

Columns I and II indicate respectively the per cent of gross and of net receipts from operation paid as taxes. Columns III and IV give similar percentages for the amount paid in taxes on corporate excess and on property assessed locally. Here of course the commutation tax is omitted. Column V indicates the proportion of the total amount going to dividends and to interest on bonds which is paid out as interest on the funded debt. The averages are for 1904 and 1905. On comparing this column with the columns III and IV it will be seen that in general the per cent paid in taxes is high as the per cent paid as interest is low, showing the effect of excluding the funded debt from the taxable valuation. Column VI gives the average amount of taxes paid on gross and net receipts, respectively, by the various companies; the average rates, 5½ per cent and 17½ per cent, paid throughout the state being taken as the rates. Columns VII and VIII are the hypothetical taxes which would have been paid on gross and net receipts, respectively, by the various companies; the average rates, 5½ per cent and 17½ per cent, paid throughout the state being taken as the rates. Column IX, the ratio of operating expenses to earnings from operation, has been added to explain the deviations of the tax on net receipts from the tax on gross receipts.

VITA.

The writer of this dissertation, Harry George Friedman, was born in 1881. Preparatory to entering college, he attended Hughes High School in Cincinnati, and was graduated in 1900. He entered the University of Cincinnati in the same year, and received the degree of bachelor of arts in 1904. During the years 1904-1907 he pursued graduate courses at Columbia University in economics and finance, sociology and statistics, political philosophy and constitutional law. His professors were E. R. A. Seligman, J. B. Clark, H. R. Seager, H. L. Moore, H. Schumacher, F. H. Giddings, W. A. Dunning, and J. W. Burgess. At the same time he was a member of the seminars conducted by Professors Seligman, Clark and Schumacher.